Atlanta at Home

Atlanta at Home

By Frances Schultz

Principal photography by Dot Griffith

WYRICK & COMPANY

Best wishes!
Frances Schultz

A Tarboro Book

Published by Wyrick & Company
Post Office Box 89
Charleston, South Carolina 29402

Set in Sabon with Gill Sans and Kuenstler Script display
Printed and bound in Korea
Designed by Sandra Strother Hudson

Library of Congress Cataloging-in-Publication Data
Schultz, Frances, 1957-
Atlanta at home / Frances Schultz
p. cm.
Includes bibliographical references and index.
ISBN 0-941711-23-4
1. Dwellings—Georgia—Atlanta. 2. Gardens—Georgia—Atlanta.
3. Atlanta (Ga.)—Buildings, structures, etc.   I. Title
F294.A88A27   1994
975.8'231—dc20   94-16928
                         CIP

All photographs in this book were taken by Dot Griffith, except
the following: pages 2–7, by Blaine-Hickey Photography, courtesy
Southern Accents magazine; pages 14–17 and page 19, by Cotton
Alston; pages 24 and 26, by Bill Hull, courtesy Atlanta History
Center; frontispiece and pages 38–41 and page 96 by Brian Gassel.

Contents

Introduction

While Atlanta today has all the trappings of a booming metropolis—big business and industry, professional sports teams, a rapid transit system, an international airport, a burgeoning population and the thrill of the Olympic Games in 1996—Atlanta is also about people—and neighborhoods. From the threads of history and diverse cultural and social influences, the city of Atlanta has woven a rich fabric of style and tradition, and nowhere is that more apparent than in the way Atlantans live at home. As modern American history scholar Kenneth Jackson once wrote, "Housing is an outward expression of the inner human nature; no society can be fully understood apart from the residences of its members."

I believe this includes all walks of "members," and that is why you will see here an elegant Buckhead landmark and a downtown warehouse studio, an elaborate formal landscape and a tiny, inner-city garden. Something about each is uniquely Atlantan. Something about each tells a story, has a history, captures a spirit. Each embraces the value and significance of a personal aesthetic and the social and cultural context in which it is cultivated. All speak of the importance of personal expression in an increasingly impersonal world.

I hope you will read this book as a record of a great city as seen through its people and their places. Because a city's beauty is more than the sum of its skyscrapers and leafy suburbs; a city's beauty lies in its soul. I hope you will glimpse it here, and find, perhaps, a new window into your own.

Frances Schultz

Acknowledgments

A great deal of the work here was done while I merely stood by and watched. Dot Griffith, primary photographer for this book, is not only a talented practitioner of her craft but a delight to schlep for and a joy to be with. And with her I was, practically joined at the hip, for a year and some. Her grace and good sense, her ready smile and her wit were, and are, an example and an inspiration. Thank you, Dot, for more than you know.

Accomplished Atlanta photographers Cotten Alston and Brian Gassel contributed photographs of Louise Allen's garden (Alston) and Benji Jones's and Laura Turner Seydel's apartments (Gassel). The Adair house photos were supplied by Hickey-Robertson Photography, courtesy *Southern Accents* magazine.

Heartfelt thanks also to the good people in this book who opened their hearts, their homes and their gardens to Dot and me and all our cameras and questions. Deepest appreciation to my editor and publisher Charles L. Wyrick, Jr. and his warm, Charleston hospitality, even on the phone.

I was lucky to have highly respected horticulturist, garden writer and good friend Martha Tate to assist in locating and writing about the gardens in this book. It would not have been possible without her. Equal gratitude goes to interior designer and friend John Oetgen, without whose taste, guidance and grace things just wouldn't have been the same.

Research was conducted through all manner of interviews and excursions through newspaper clips and various books and magazines, but I am indebted to Franklin Garrett and his *Atlanta and Environs,* volumes I and II, and to Harold H. Martin for his volume III of that series. Also invaluable was *Classic Atlanta,* by William Mitchell and Van Jones Martin, and Elizabeth Meredith Dowling's *American Classicist.* Able editorial and research assistance was provided by Lilly Varn.

Thank you to those who were especially helpful in getting this project off the ground, encouraging me, and in some cases reading the manuscript when it was finished: Vee Adair, Louise Allen, Dottie Fuqua, Brooks Garcia, Paige Henry, Comer Jennings and Spencer Tunnell. Jim Landon did all of the above, and still managed to look after the legal matters and fix lunch in Highlands, too. Bless him.

Then there is a special group without whom I might not ever have even begun this book, much less finished it. Among them are teachers, mentors and friends—some from way back—who gave me a chance, urged me on, told me I could, or taught me what I needed to know eventually to know how to do this project: Lillian Spears, Don Roberts, Martha Steger, Ann Gray, Lorna Wyckoff, Andy Spalding, Bob Steed, Gina Schreiber and Chris Madden. And thanks to Sherrill Holt, who invited me to Atlanta for a weekend; five years later, I'm still here.

And finally, there is the handful of family and friends who, for what seems like forever to them and to me, always managed with sincere interest to ask, "How's the book?" And always took time to listen: Ruth Clark, Duvall and Rex Fuqua, Mary Bray, George Cox, Karon Cullen, Farrar Martin, Howell Morrison, Bettie Bearden Pardee, Marshall Persinger, H, Sherrie Rollins, Candy Sheehan, Anne Sterchi and Camille Wright.

Atlanta at Home

The Adair Residence on West Paces Ferry Road

*M*r. and Mrs. Augustus Dixon Adair III are of a rare species called "Old Atlantans:" this does not refer to their ages. Mr. Adair's ancestors came to Atlanta before the Civil War, and his great grandfather was one of the city's early mayors. The Adairs are as fond of their memories of living in Atlanta as they are of those recorded while living away from it—which they did, for nearly twenty years—in Venezuela, Spain and Italy, where Mr. Adair headed international operations of a large manufacturing company. Mrs. Adair is an accomplished portraitist and is the author of a book about eighteenth century pastel portrait artists. The couple have three grown children and are active in a number of community projects.

Once, on a visit home from Madrid, they bought the house they knew they would eventually return to, a house evocative of the European architecture they loved, but on the land of their American forefathers. Designed in 1919 by architect Philip Thornton Marye, the Renaissance revival stucco residence stands on a broad carpet of grass, shaded by mighty oaks and caressed by creeping tendrils of ivy, wisteria and honeysuckle. The interiors,

A stately presence on West Paces Ferry Road, the Adairs' stucco Renaissance revival residence was designed in 1919 by architect P. Thornton Marye. Opposite: Soft light bathes the morning room and highlights its coffered ceiling. A family portrait by Mrs. Adair rests on an easel in the corner.

framed in intricate moldings and carefully crafted architectural detail, reflect the best from both sides of the Atlantic and this side of the Mason-Dixon.

Fine southern houses of yore were predominantly furnished with English pieces, and the Adairs' respective families had passed them along. Their treasures acquired abroad are mostly Italian and French, from the seventeenth to the nineteenth centuries. The art, books and decorative accessories were chosen sometimes for their provenance, sometimes simply for their interesting shapes. It is an assemblage of objects from the exquisite to the exquisitely obscure. In the library, which Mrs. Adair says she has "mixed and mingled" lots of unrelated reminders of their travels. A stately Sung Dynasty figure stares coldly across the room at a rare, bronze crawling Krishna—an image of the Hindu god as a child already enlightened. The same room displays with equal prominence an unusual musical instrument from Indonesia, a roof tile from Pompeii, and a Buddha from Ankor Wat. An early eighteenth-century Venetian settee stands next to a hall gallery filled with what

A handsome, carved mantelpiece frames an Aubusson-upholstered French canapé and supports a bust of Marie Antoinette. The crystal and bronze doré chandelier is believed to have belonged to Catherine the Great.

the owner calls "a lot of unexplained wooden pieces." Those explainable, however, include a beautiful, mirrored Peruvian picture frame and Greek icons possibly dating to the fifteenth century. The drawing room chandelier once belonged to Catherine the Great.

Two portraits by Alexander Roslin and a Martin Van Mytens work of the Empress Maria Theresa of Austria highlight an art collection also graced by pastels of the Adair children, done by Mrs. Adair. She points out that Maria Theresa's gaze is toward one of her own children, a porcelain bust of her flighty daughter, Marie Antoinette, which adorns a nearby mantelpiece. The young queen, however, looks away, ignoring her. Chides Mrs. Adair, "If she'd listened to her mother, she might not have lost her head!"

With a twinkle in its eye, a glint of amusement at the world it embraces, the Adairs' is a gracious home that both reflects and embodies the spirit of its owners. The house has the soul of an artist, sensitive to its own visual

A Martin Van Mytens portrait of Empress Maria Theresa, wife of Holy Roman Emperor Francis I, commands the expansive foyer. A gilded antique harp and Aubusson carpet are spare but exquisite decoration.

Mrs. Adair designed her dining table by marrying a pair of Venetian consoles to a long center section. Two mirrors, centered by the bronze doré chandelier, enhance the room's symmetry.

On the mantel, a Sung Dynasty figure is flanked by a pair of Indian temple carvings and reflected in a Chippendale mirror. Olive-colored walls complement the reddish and rose tones in the Aubusson.

In the morning room, a pastel portrait by Mrs. Adair of a family member in period dress hangs above an array of porcelain boxes, paper weights and other treasures. The bookcase holds vellum-covered volumes from the 17th century.

rhythm. Rooms copiously furnished and accessorized are balanced with those more spare, and in between are the broad expanses of entrance hall and stairway. "I've always done that," Mrs. Adair says. "I like to fill every available space . . . and then have a cool area, where the eye can rest."

Virginia Adair—called "Vee" by her friends—remembers when the busy thoroughfare on which she lives was once a dirt road. "People were always talking about it," she recalls. During the days of the Indians, it was the primary highway north of Atlanta, leading west to the river. In the 1830s, Hardy Pace established a ferry crossing the Chattahoochee River that remained in operation until 1904, when the traffic became too much for it to bear and a bridge was built. Residential development spread north to Ansley Park and farther out to Buckhead. In 1911 the James L. Dickey, Sr., estate released 303 acres along Paces Ferry Road to the Tuxedo Park Company, which divided it into enormous lots. Prime location, gently rolling terrain and cool, wooded areas made "the dirt road" highly desirable, and some of Atlanta's best-known citizens made their homes there and still do. Today, West Paces Ferry Road boasts the Governor's Mansion, the French consulate, the home of Anne Cox Chambers, and the Neel Reid/Philip Shutze-designed "Pink Palace," a 1923 baroque revival villa also known as the Calhoun-Thornwell house. "We used to drive out here on Sundays to see the pretty houses, particularly the Calhouns', because they had such a gorgeous vista," recalls Mr. Adair. The exalted vista, which once swept over a hundred acres or so, has since been encroached upon by Northside Parkway at what used to be one boundary of the property and by streets and houses at every other.

Inevitably, the same is true for the Adairs. Years ago, when the Lindsey Hopkinses owned the house, it was surrounded by forty acres. Mr. Adair remembers that, as a young man, he used to swim and play tennis there. But where the tennis court and pool once were, is now a paved public street. Where the old driveway began, the French consulate now stands. Still, the history, prestige and dignity of West Paces Ferry Road has withstood the onslaught of progress and remains a favorite of Sunday drivers to this day.

The Anne Cox Chambers House

*T*he home of Anne Cox Chambers is a classic white brick English Regency residence with distinctive arched niches, painted red, flanking the front door. It is across from the Governor's Mansion on West Paces Ferry Road and next door to the white clapboard manse Neel Reid designed for Mr. and Mrs. James Dickey. On a street of high profile Atlantans, present and past, Anne Cox Chambers is certainly one of the highest. A gracious benefactor of numerous arts and charitable organizations, Chambers is chairman of Atlanta Newspapers and a director of the newspapers' corporate parent, Cox Enterprises. The burgeoning, multi-billion-dollar com-

Behind a George III satinwood writing table, Anne Cox Chambers works in a sunny office adjacent to her bedroom. Opposite: Architect Shutze called this dining salon one of his "most celebrated rooms." It is today essentially as he created it in 1929, in the Chinese Chippendale style which was popular during the Regency period.

munications company now headquartered in Atlanta, was founded in Ohio by Chambers' father James C. Cox, a former governor of Ohio and, in 1920, a presidential candidate with Franklin D. Roosevelt as his running mate. In 1939, Cox bought *The Atlanta Journal*, and in 1950, *The Atlanta Constitution*, afternoon and morning papers, respectively.

Today, ·while Chambers calls Atlanta home, she is also a citizen of the world. She served as ambassador to Belgium under President Jimmy Carter from 1977 to 1981; and in 1993, she was awarded the French Legion of Honor by President François Mitterrand. A diminutive woman of formidable presence, Chambers has entertained, and been entertained by, some of the world's most powerful politicians, distinguished statesmen and sought-after celebrities.

Nevertheless, about twenty-five years ago, soon after she moved into the house, Chambers was more than a little anxious at the prospect of receiving for the first time a certain visitor for dinner. "I was very nervous about his reaction," she recalls. The visitor was Philip Trammell Shutze, who some fifty years before had designed the house, and who for fifty years hence and everafter will be revered in Atlanta as creator of some of the region's most lovely and graceful buildings, and as the architect of *Swan House*. "So, basically, I didn't do—and wouldn't have done—anything to change what Mr. Shutze had done structurally. But I would say the decor was much more formal before." With silks, linens, cottons, fresh florals and toiles, and pale, clear washes of color, the look of the house now is no less elegant than that of its predecessor, but it is decidedly less formal, and airier. It is, quite simply, exquisite. Mr. Shutze apparently approved of every aspect but one: "He pointed with his cane," Chambers recalls, "at the entrance hall stair with the black, Victorian flowered carpet which I had intended to replace but had not yet done so." "That," the man glowered, "must go."

Shutze died in 1982, but one speculates he might approve of the leopard print laid over the curving, suspended stairway today, and that the house through its several re-doings would satisfy him still. Several years ago an electrical fire swept through the house, leaving the structure intact but destroying the fabrics and furniture. The venerable New York decorating firm

Glazed celadon-colored walls set off a Brunschwig & Fils chintz at the windows and on the sofa. The end tables are 19th-century English.

McMillen was called in, and a young staff designer, who just happened to be from Atlanta and home for a visit, was put to the task. Brooks Anderson continued to work with Chambers until his death in late 1993, and he came to admire very much his special client's taste and style.

The living room, Anderson said, is his client's epitome. "I love that room because it's so *her*," he explained. "She doesn't like brocades or damasks, or super-rich, shiny looking fabrics. She likes them much more subdued and restrained. I was surprised she went for the velvet pillows." Ivory woven linen covers sofas and chairs in which are propped antiqued velvet pillows the shade of a dusty rose. A butter-and-cream Fortuny cotton print is on French fauteuils. A small watercolor by Marc Chagall hangs discreetly in a corner. French, English Regency, and lacquered Chinoiserie pieces blend seamlessly within walls glazed a pale, glowing yellow. Indeed the painted surfaces of this house are among its most sublime subtleties, and they are the stroke of New Yorker Dino Pfund.

Attributable to Anderson's respect for balance, proportion and scale, and enhanced by architecture that is a paragon of the same, the almost-delicate, luminous quality of the living room is reflected throughout the house without ever becoming fragile or flighty. Porcelains in subtle, muted tones or clear, bright colors complement paintings by such artists as John Singer Sargent, Milton Avery, Toulouse-Lautrec, Pablo Picasso and Marc Chagall. Also in abundance—as dinner guest Audrey Hepburn once told her upon observing they "liked all the same things"—are "lots of flowers and dogs, both living and on the walls." At any given time, several canine companions are in residence. In the foyer stands a bronze terrier sculpture which once belonged to Queen Victoria. Fabrics are from a palette of celadon, fern, daffodil, berry and bisque. It is a palette from nature, quiet and harmonious— an ivory, pale green and rust chintz in the morning room; a yellow, unlined

In Mrs. Chambers' bedroom, all is yellow and light. Unlined silk curtains are paired with woven wooden shades. The rug is a 19th-century Ouschak.

Architect Philip Shutze's love for symmetry is duly honored by the living room decor. A quartet of French Empire feuteuils covered in a Fortuny print define two seating areas. Rare, yellow Faience porcelain is displayed in niches on either side of the window.

silk print at the bedroom windows; and in her adjacent study, a custom-colored toile to echo the glaze of the bedroom walls.

And, as it flows perfectly with the rest of the house, the dining room has remained much as Shutze designed it. He had the wallpaper made in China, especially for the room. The doors on either side of the fireplace, one false and one leading to the sun room, he painted a warm persimmon. "He was quite an old man by the time we lived here," Chambers recalls, "and when he came for dinner, sometimes he would stand at the door to the dining room and say, 'It's one of my most celebrated rooms.'"

Chambers is generous with her house, opening it often for the benefit of various causes and candidates. "I enjoy sharing it," she says, and as Mr. Shutze told her himself, she has "brought the house to life."

Louise Allen's Garden

A large tract of land on Northside Drive has been in the Richardson family since the early part of the century, when anything north of West Paces Ferry was considered "way out in the country." Today Northside Drive is a busy thoroughfare, and members and descendants of the Richardson family have built and lived here all along—since the early 1920s. Here, Louise Richardson Allen, wife of the illustrious former mayor Ivan Allen, Jr., has for more than forty years nurtured a garden that is a lot like the Allens themselves. There is nothing flashy about it; there is subtlety and refinement and integrity. Begun in plantings around the house and worked from there, the garden's naturalized scheme reflects a love for the beauty of individual plants beyond their value as decoration. And while there are

A bank brims with pink azaleas, dogwood and pieris, planted amid a rock garden. Opposite: The Allen house may be the only example of Cape Dutch architecture in Atlanta. Hydrangeas in the foreground are a profusion of purple.

The walled garden is behind the house and a lovely view from the living room and back terrace. Pink coneflowers, yellow daylilies and Russian sage brighten a corner near the gate.

indeed great seasonal shows, this garden is best taken as a whole, rather than as the sum of its parts. Loosely framed vignettes of unusual plant collections, a rock garden, and rare trees are enveloped in a park-like setting blessed with a sweeping view of meadow and woods and an occasional meandering goose or two. "We are so fortunate to have inherited this view," Allen says. "We can see it from almost anywhere in the house, and it's so peaceful."

Among these verdant acres of peace are native and species azaleas, rhododendrons, viburnums, hydrangeas, fothergillas, forsythias, a rare native stewartia, and one franklinia tree. And while there are a host of herbaceous perennials in the walled garden off the back terrace, Allen says, "If I had my druthers, I'd rather have rare trees." Indeed, she does have rare trees, two copper beeches and a cutleaf beech among them. And she has trees which were rare when she acquired them but which are more widely available today. "And I think that's wonderful," she adds. Her Japanese maples, for example, are prizes, and some are forty-five years old. She has also for years had golden barberry and pieris, the latter esteemed as a shrub deer do not eat. And though both plants have recently begun to appear more frequently in the southeast, Allen spotted them nearly thirty years ago—the chartreuse-colored barberry at Wisley gardens in England and the *Pieris japonica* in a Hudson River valley garden. Her twenty-five-year-old Kousa dogwood (*Cornus kousa*) is also a favorite, its erratic blooming habits notwithstanding. "Don't give up on it," she advises good-naturedly. Less temperamental and more common Georgia natives are the sourwood trees planted along the circular drive in front of the house. Their cream-colored panicles in June and golden-red leaves in October arrive as surely as the seasons themselves.

In early spring, the new growth of the Japanese maples accompanies the blooming of native azalea, several varieties of viburnum, and philadelphus (mock orange). Following are the rhododendron, peonies, hosta, clematis, Japanese roof iris, and baptisia. Toward June and into early summer come the oakleaf hydrangeas, then the blue macrophylla hydrangeas, the white Annabelle, and the lacecaps, which are sometimes pink and sometimes blue. Astilbes, ferns, daylilies, Japanese sword fern and red native lobelia are

Native yellow flame azaleas and a rare double-flowering native dogwood frame this view toward the walled garden. A Japanese cherry tree blooms in the background.

planted in and among rocks and trees and banksides. Later in summer a large butterfly bush (buddleia) and yellow hypericum splash bright color near a side door. A lantana, just this side of garish, preens on the terrace.

Allen constantly seeks knowledge and inspiration from all sources, from other gardens and other countries. Her interest in ornamental trees stems from a trip to England in the 1960s, when she was taken with a paperbark maple at *Stourhead*. A visit to South Africa prompted the architectural renovation of the house after Cape Dutch style, designed by Atlanta architect Henri Jova. And frequent sojourns to friends' gardens and nurseries only encourage her apparently incurable botanical acquisitiveness—although she does not buy a plant for its particular effect in the landscape. She buys it and then finds a place for it. "There is no plan. I just plunk things around," she laughs. "But nature has a way of blending things together, doesn't it?"

And, without meaning to, Louise Allen plunks herself amid a metaphor. While the garden is a metaphor for many things in life, the same may be said of one's *approach* to the garden. It applies to Allen and to her husband as well. As nature will inevitably blend things together, the quality of the outcome may be enhanced by the equanimity of its facilitator. Ivan Allen's two terms as mayor of Atlanta reckoned with the worst of the civil rights strife in the South and the best in the building and development of the South's "premier city." And in so doing, Mayor Allen earned a respectful place in history—Atlanta's and the nation's. Responsible for the integration of the City Hall cafeteria and the first to hire black people for prominent positions in city government, Allen recognized that the progress of the city depended on its ability "to blend things together"—and that meant people, too. In 1964 he testified before Congress in support of the Civil Rights Act. Two sweltering summers later, he walked unarmed and virtually unprotected into the streets of the Summerhill riots. On the night of April 4, 1968, when Martin Luther King was assassinated in Memphis, he drove to the Kings' home in Atlanta to offer condolences and begin the managing of yet another crisis. Mrs. Allen went with him.

Louise Allen's public life by his side was, and is, consistent with her private one. In her volunteer efforts and civic work, her words and deeds have

Amid the early spring finery of her garden, Louise Allen weeds and watches for new growth.

The Allens' beloved meadow, bright with fall foliage, is a pleasant resting place for geese heading south for the winter.

emanated from an unequivocal sense of equality. In 1970 she was named Atlanta's Woman of the Year. In 1993 the Atlanta Historical Society dedicated its new Museum of Atlanta History to her, as she is considered the driving force behind the Society's growth and rise to national stature. She is also the niece of the late Edward Inman, builder of *Swan House*, which the Society bought in 1967 to use as its headquarters. They wanted to name the museum for her, but she wouldn't hear of it. She eschews such symbolic gestures of aggrandizement, as she did when a newspaper reporter once suggested that her family defined the best of Old Atlanta, while her husband's was the best of New Atlanta. "I, for one, have never thought about it," she replied, smiling. Louise Allen's life, like her garden, is cultivated not in the power of elitism but in the strength and magnanimity of inclusion.

Swan House

*M*any Atlanta stories may be told through *Swan House*. There is the story of the preeminent Atlanta family who built it and the extraordinary architect who designed it. And there is history—how Atlanta has developed and how it continues to grow. How appropriate it is, then, that the Atlanta Historical Society was once headquartered in *Swan House*, and that the grand old house today is at the heart of the Atlanta History Center.

The architect responsible is Philip Trammell Shutze, and there is an excellent and definitive book about him entitled *American Classicist* (1989, Riz-

In the morning room, tiny swans carved into the capitals of the pilasters flanking the fireplace are typical of the meticulous architectural detail throughout the house. **Opposite: Comissioned by Mr. and Mrs. Edward H. Inman and completed in 1928,** *Swan House* **is a crowning achievement of exalted Atlanta architect Philip Trammell Shutze and is today at the heart of the Atlanta History Center.**

zoli), written by an Atlantan, Elizabeth Meredith Dowling. *Swan House* is probably the most well known and lasting memorial to the architect's considerable body of work, comprising predominantly residential designs but including commercial projects as well. His personality was equally unconstrained, and the architect was alternately amusing and abrasive in his freespoken and sometimes caustic candor. A native of Columbus, Georgia, with degrees in architecture from the Georgia Institute of Technology and Columbia University, Shutze was awarded the prestigious Rome Prize in 1915 and studied in Italy. In Atlanta he associated with the firm of Hentz, Reid and Adler, becoming partner and chief designer after Neel Reid's death in 1926, and the firm became Hentz, Adler and Shutze. His most prolific period was during the 1920s and 1930s, and it was during that time when he designed *Swan House*.

Two years and approximately $200,000 in the making, *Swan House* was

In the dining room is a stunning pair of Chippendale carved swan consoles, attributed to Thomas Johnson. Decorator Ruby Ross Wood lent a hand to *Swan House*, although architect Philip Shutze had strong opinions about interior appointments.

completed in 1928 as the new home of Mr. and Mrs. Edward H. Inman. Inman inherited substantial wealth from his father Hugh T. Inman, who at one time operated one of the largest cotton brokerages in the world. Mrs. Inman had a fondness for swans, hence the name of the house and a recurring motif throughout it.

Shutze did not write much about his architecture, presuming perhaps that it spoke for itself—which indeed it did and most eloquently. So his rare,

The magnificent Italian baroque garden facade of *Swan House* faces Andrews Drive in Buckhead.

written description of *Swan House* as it appears in Dowling's book is best not paraphrased: "There was no attempt to adhere slavishly to any predetermined style or period for the design of the Inman House as to exterior, interior, furnishing and landscaping. Generally speaking, the house may be placed in the first quarter, or better, the first half of the eighteenth century. It was the owner's desire that this be done . . ." Mrs. Inman was an admirer of the English architect William Kent and his early eighteenth-century takes on Andrea Palladio's sixteenth-century designs; Shutze's most propitious inclination was toward the Italian baroque. So, naturally and fortuitously, *Swan House* represents a marriage of classical forms in an early twentieth-century context, and the style of the house is referred to as classical.

A formal boxwood garden off of one wing of the house, writes Dowling, "hides the transition from the Italian baroque garden façade to the startlingly different William Kent entry façade . . . To reflect the dual stylistic nature of the house, Shutze composed a landscape conceived from Italian themes and filtered through English experience." Referring to this design, Shutze wrote, "As to the landscaping, whatever has been done was with the Italian garden in England in mind. Before the advent of Capability Brown, as in the Italian vernacular, there are not perennial flower borders as such; an architectural framework with evergreen planting is the order . . ."

True to Shutze's observation not "to adhere slavishly to any predetermined style," the interior decoration is not as formal as the house itself, reflecting a more modern and, at the time, stylish, English country house look. The '20s and '30s were the heyday of Elsie de Wolfe and her cohorts,

Bespeaking light, symmetry and grace, this porch wing of *Swan House* looks onto a formal boxwood garden.

one of whom was Georgia native Ruby Ross Wood, who worked with the Inmans on *Swan House* as she had in their previous home in Ansley Park. Shutze, too, concerned himself with interiors, and *Swan House* was no exception. The round, open-ended hall with its Ionic order columns and black and white marble floor opens to four public rooms on the main floor and culminates in "a splendid circular staircase with bronze ballustrade and walnut treads, fine carved doors and overdoors and ornamental plaster. Consoles, paintings, screens are noteworthy."

In the dining room are a Queen Anne molded ceiling, Aubusson rug, Chinoiserie wallpaper, and bright plaid silk draperies—the result of Mrs. Inman's desire expressed to Wood that she have at her windows "the colors of the rainbow." Most extraordinary in the room, however, are the pair of Chippendale carved swan consoles, attributed to Thomas Johnson. The rich architectural detail owes partly to the superlative crafting of English carver H. J. Millard, whose work Shutze describes thusly: in the library, "Wrenlike panelling, with trims, cornices, overdoors and archivolts carved to accord with the Grinling Gibbons style of decorations of the mantel and over mantel." And in the "elegant morning room . . . engaged Corinthian columns on pedestals with capitals adorned with diminutive swans."

Mr. Inman died less than three years after the house was completed. Mrs. Inman continued to live there with her son and his family, until she died in 1965. The Atlanta Historical Society acquired the property from her estate, as was her wish, but among her heirs are grandchildren, nieces and nephews still living in Atlanta who remember roaring around the house as children and who recall what great style this grand lady had. Philip Shutze died in 1982 at the age of ninety-two, bequeathing to the Atlanta Historical Society his personal research library and his precious collections of Chinese export porcelain, European ceramics and silver, rugs, paintings, furniture and other decorative objects from China, England, and America, now housed in *Swan House* and the History Center's library.

The Museum of Atlanta History opened in October of 1993 and is the latest addition to the thirty-two-acre complex that is the Atlanta History Center. In addition to *Swan House* there is the Tullie Smith Farm, comprising

Opposite the garden facade is the dramatically contrasting entry, inspired by English architect William Kent's interpretations of Palladian architecture.

an 1840s farmhouse, garden and blacksmith shop through which visitors can learn what life was really like in the antebellum era. The surrounding grounds include formal gardens, wooded nature trails, native plants and flowering trees and shrubs, a quarry, and an international Garden for Peace. Events held throughout the year range from educational lectures and symposia, to a storytelling festival, to the grand annual *Swan House* Ball. Candlelight Tours, organized by the Society's Members Guild, are a Christmas-time favorite during which the two houses and History Center grounds are decorated and open in the evening for strolling carolers, gospel choirs, living history exhibits, and other festive goings-on. The hundreds of candles lit for the occasion might symbolize points of light the Atlanta Historical Society has kindled, shining in its role as steward and archive of the spirit of this city.

The Governor's Mansion

It was nearly a hundred years after Atlanta became the capital of Georgia that state citizens decided to build an official residence for its chief executive. Having derided the erstwhile Ansley Park mansion—a looming, granite bungalow on The Prado—as "cold, gray, austere, and medieval," state lawmakers in 1961 resolved to form a committee to study the building of a new, presumably less gloomy, gubernatorial abode. A bill approving the financing was approved the following year, and in 1966 the neoclassical

David Byers served as consultant for the mansion's interior decoration. The exquisite window treatment in the state dining room is exemplary of Byers's taste and attention to detail.

Opposite: The main entry adjoins a circular stair hall which leads to the governor's family residence. By the door to the state dining room, a bust of Benjamin Franklin by Jean Antoine Houdon commands a place of importance. Franklin was Georgia's colonial agent to the Court of St. James.

anathema to "austere and medieval" stood completed. In its red-bricked, Doric-columned glory, the new 24,000-square-foot-mansion was a symbol of the New South but still in keeping with its old southern heritage.

Atlanta was not always the capital of Georgia. From 1807 until 1868, Milledgeville held the honor and boasted a governor's mansion which to this day is considered a masterwork of classical revival architecture. But by the end of the Civil War, Atlanta had grown tremendously and was more accessible by rail than was Milledgeville. So, when the 1868 Constitutional Convention met—a requirement of all secessionist states for restoration to the Union—the City Council of Atlanta proposed to make their city the state capital. The proposal was accepted. City Hall became the Capitol, and a handsome private residence on the corner of Peachtree and Cain streets became the governor's mansion. The years took their toll on the house, however, and in 1923 it was demolished to make way for the Henry Grady Hotel, which was also later demolished. The seventy-story Peachtree Plaza Hotel now stands on the site. The executive residence moved from Peachtree Street to The Prado in Ansley Park, to a thirteen-room, granite manse built by Edwin P. Ansley himself. And there it remained until the state legislature deemed fit to erect an official governor's mansion, some forty-two years later.

It fades from memory that the 1966 decision was not an easy one. The vote in the legislature was by no means unanimous, and the political fight over it was fierce. Ironically, among the leaders in favor of the mansion was a governor who would never be able to live in it; and vehement opposition was vented from one who would. These adversaries were then-Governor Carl Sanders and then-State Senator Jimmy Carter. Amid the maelstrom, however, the resolution was approved and eighteen acres of the Robert F. Maddox estate on West Paces Ferry Road was acquired as the site. In 1968, the mansion was dedicated and Governor Lester Maddox (no relation to Robert F.) moved in—fitting, somehow, that the mansion be as controversial as the first man to live in it.

When the doors were opened, the interior was nothing near the "cold and gray" of its predecessor. Assembled there was, and is, a world-class collection of early nineteenth-century neoclassical antiques and decorative objects for which the people of Georgia have much to be proud and many to thank. Undertaking the task of the building and furnishing was a Fine Arts Committee comprising seventy-six Georgia citizens with expertise and influence in every pertinent area, from engineering to art history. Chairing this committee was Henry D. Green, a native Georgian and preeminent authority on Southern art and antiques. It was Green who painstakingly

searched for and selected the mansion's art and furnishings, and the result of his efforts is considered possibly to be the finest American Federal collection in the country. The committee favored the period, approximately 1775 to 1830, because it was a prosperous era in Georgia history, a time when its agriculturally-based economy thrived. The architecture, too, was appropriate to the period and a complement to the terraced parterre garden. Though this garden is not visible from the street, it is the focus of the formal landscape, still much in its original form.

The size and decor of the rooms are deftly varied to accommodate the demands of formal receptions and state occasions while simultaneously functioning as a family home. The state reception hall and drawing room, for example, are rather grandly scaled and formal, while the library and family dining room are smaller and more intimate. Throughout the house, most of the pieces are American and attributed to the finest cabinetmakers, such as Duncan Phyfe. Of the choice works by European artists is a bust of Benjamin Franklin by French sculptor Jean Antoine Houdon. (Before the American Revolution, Franklin represented Georgia as a colonial agent to the Court of St. James.) Historic value attaches to many pieces in the mansion, and the growing repertoire of contemporary anecdotes—the favorite painting of one governor, the lamp nearly smashed by the child of another—reflects the inhabitants' appreciation for their temporary home.

These stories and others were fondly recalled at a luncheon honoring Henry Green in the spring of 1992. Assembled there were many surviving members of the original Fine Arts Committee and every governor living who had occupied the new mansion, one of whom became president. Former President Carter spoke briefly, and recanted his previous objections to the mansion with grace and good humor. "I'm very glad I was voted down," he said, and continued by expressing gratitude to Governor Sanders for establishing the quality and integrity of the committee. That there have been very few changes to the mansion since then, he said, "is a testimony to the quality of what was done at the beginning." And what the people of Georgia have now "is not just a governor's mansion, but a museum for the South and the nation."

The Georgia governor's mansion was completed in 1968 and stands on the site of the former Maddox estate on West Paces Ferry Road. Aspects of the original landscape have been well preserved.

A terraced, formal landscape is the classical complement to the Greek revival architecture of the mansion.

The Pattersons on Peachtree Battle Avenue

*W*here the home of Sallie and J. O. Patterson now stands, many a Civil War soldier stood also, and fought and died. Peachtree Battle Avenue is named for the Battle of Peachtree Creek, a grueling and pivotal late-summer conflict in the siege of Atlanta that led to Mayor James M. Calhoun's surrender of the city to General William T. Sherman on September 2, 1864. The war ended seven months later. A memorial to the Peachtree Creek battle was erected 100 years later, in 1964, when the country was again torn apart by civil strife, fighting a war halfway around the world in Vietnam and trying desperately to resolve its conflicts at home.

In this evocative context of history, it is refreshing to find a modern home in which some of the good of history is preserved in the continuance of certain traditional customs—such as seated dinners and dressing for the occasion. In this day and age it is unusual to hear someone say, "We do not entertain informally," and yet that is precisely what Sallie Patterson will tell you.

Built in the mid-1930s, the sedate, red brick Georgian house is nearly hidden from the street by a manicured holly hedge and a pair of stately, monumental magnolias. Having undergone several phases of remodeling, the last two under the watchful and well-trained eye of the late designer James Boyd Young, the house is most definitely a grown-up house, for grown-up parties, pretty flower arrangements and perpetually plumped-up pillows. While the decor is decidedly formal, incorporating French, English and Italian antiques, eighteenth- and ninetenth-century paintings, and swaths of silk, damask, brocade, and cut velvet, Patterson and Young nonetheless strove to keep it from becoming starchy. When they began work, she says, "It was really hard for me to articulate what I wanted—so Jim just started coming in with fabrics and colors. I think after a while we were both picking out the same things and eliminated a lot of middle ground. We loved

the airy silks for the draperies, for instance, and he knew I didn't like chintz. We wanted the look to be rich, but mellow. And I always felt like there shouldn't be a chair or piece of furniture in the whole house that doesn't invite someone to sit down and prop her feet up if she wants to, and no dish that can't hold a cigarette. You know there's not anything more important than your friends and how they feel when they're here. It's just a house until you get the people in it; then it's a home."

The dining room seats sixteen, and often does. It, like the living room opposite, is appointed in muted, misty tones of beige, cream, pale yellow, smoke and sky. The architectural details—the panels and moldings in both these rooms—were designed by Young, as was the marble floor in the foyer. The fireplace mantels he bought in France. The bar and card room, to which the gentlemen retreat after dinner for brandy and cigars, are credited to Young and Mr. Patterson, as is the stunning wine cellar. They are the

The sheen and texture of silk take many forms in this opulent living room, elegantly finished with a Lacey Champion rug and gleaming Oriental table.

masculine areas of the house, dark and handsome. Unequivocally feminine are the two guest bedrooms, furnished in predominantly French antiques. In pale shades of yellow, apricot, and olive, gently draped and perfectly trimmed silks have a subtle sheen that reflects a deference to fineness and delicacy—a nearly lost art in this era of wash-and-wear, rough-and-ready, no maintenance everything. Nor is the owner anxious to change it constantly, or to make it "new" again and again. "If a fabric cannot be replaced, I'll find the next closest thing. I'm not really crazy about change. I think we've created a soft, elegant, comfortable feeling, and it's exactly the way I like it. To me, it's forever." And, too, it is a willingness to accept permanence in one's life, to show an appreciation for and a security in one's circumstances, one's station in life. It is, perhaps, an acceptance of one's own history and what is good about it.

The Pattersons' upstairs guest bedroom is as rich and comforting as its colors imply: butter and cream.

The L. Benjamin Jones Apartment in Buckhead

There is a longstanding joke around the South that whether one is going to heaven or hell, one must first change planes in Atlanta. A similar joke around Buckhead is that whether one is going to a new house, different marital status, or another stage in life, one must first change residences at The Paces. Built in 1974, The Paces has become a discreet, though architecturally unremarkable, landmark. Whether the landmark survives, and for how long, remains to be seen by the year 2018, when the fifty-year land lease expires, and control of the property reverts to the original owners.

The buildings belong to a local management company, but the land is held by the venerable John W. Grant family. A gently sloping thirty acres planted in oaks, dogwoods, azaleas and laurels, the choice parcel was at one time part of the family's 112-acre Buckhead estate (its notable legacy is a handsome Tudor mansion fronting West Paces Ferry Road, sold in 1956 to the Cherokee Town and Country Club). From a development standpoint, the Paces are a buffer between the affluent, big-house part of Buckhead and its commercial and less expensive areas. It is a misconception that all houses in Buckhead are mansions. Indeed, much of the building during the fifties and sixties was of a more modest ilk, small brick and clapboard single-family houses now fast being converted for commercial use. But it is precisely these side-street clusters of restaurants, boutiques, garden shops and hair salons that enhance the appeal of the area and retain its neighborhood flavor, no mean feat in a sprawling place like Atlanta—once accused of being "a forest looking for a city." On weekends, Buckhead swarms with party-seeking young people, and the streets and sidewalks are lively and crowded.

Fortunately for Paces residents, they are right in the middle of this popular grazing and shopping enclave. For former resident L. Benjamin Jones, the third floor apartment proved a satisfactory home, office and laboratory for his solo interior design business. His seven-year experiment in it went from heavy, gilt-ridden, English and overdone, to a lighter, brighter and more pared-down redemption of its former self. But no less elegant. His work for clients, including the Carl F. Allens, the Fred Aliases, the Michael Crawfords and the Southern Center for International Studies, has evolved similarly.

Jones's Paces apartment illustrates a mélange of influences, bedecked as it is in one room with Scalamandré silks, cut velvets and French porcelains,

Jewel tones in pillows, porcelains and accessories shimmer against the muted backgrounds of upholstery, carpet and wall color, while bringing out the deeper shades in the antique painted screen.

In the den, a simple black and white ticking stripe combined with touches of paisley, plaid, bouclé and blue and white porcelain create a cozy alcove. Sketches and works on paper are hung with double strands of chain from a picture rail.

and relaxed in another with striped cotton ticking, a worn leather chaise, old books and the odd bronzed baby shoe or other bibelot with special meaning, if not high style.

Jones confesses there are times when he'd like to be rid of the clutter—have just one, wonderful piece of art on a table—but he can't bring himself to it. Though Jones has since moved to Midtown and scaled down his decor somewhat, his Paces apartment is both a history and a statement of where he was, artistically, at that time. It is a freeze-frame in the evolution of an aesthetic—and his response to the forces that shape it. One constant, however, is color; if Jones's style has a trademark, this is it. "Though I'm lighter handed with it now than I used to be," he says. "Maybe that's a sign of the times." In the living room, Jones's palette is of clear, fresh colors, like the jellybeans he keeps in pretty compotes and containers around the room. In the den and kitchen are neutrals accented with color; and in the bedroom are deep, soothing hues, like those in an interesting landscape. "Color in a room leaves it open to new things," Jones says, "and when you're adding things to your life—even if it's just books or magazines—they look like they fit."

The Garden of Nancy and Holcombe Green

When Atlanta plantsman and garden designer Ryan Gainey talks about gardens, he doesn't just talk about flowers and shrubs, he talks about history, philosophy and the importance of being correct. The garden of Nancy and Holcombe Green in Buckhead is one of the finest in the southeast, he believes, because it fulfills the most important criteria: It is properly set, historically appropriate, and the philosophical idea is correct. It embraces the architecture of the house and seamlessly integrates into the hard-

Oakleaf hydrangeas adrift among English ivy make a gracious presentation in a shady front garden. A cryptomeria stands tall with the chimney, and Hills of Snow hydrangeas bloom along the house. Opposite: The low, stone wall around the swimming pool is planted with fall-blooming pink daisy mums, salvia, sedum and soft silver artemisia.

wood setting so typical of Atlanta and the Piedmont region. The garden looks simply as if it were allowed to grow that way, rather than contrived for effect. "We didn't want it to be terribly formal," says Mrs. Green. "We felt the garden should look natural and as if it's always been there, and Ryan is wonderful at that."

As with a good, traditional garden, the Greens' is a series of garden rooms which is a continuation of the house, the architecture and the taste of the people who live there. There is no single plant or feature which screams "Look at me!" nor are any garden accoutrements obtrusive. When the

The stunning formal rose garden is bordered in boxwood and candytuft, with foxgloves spiking the perimeter.

Fine carved compotes from France are handsome complements to the stonework of the shady terrace.

Greens acquired the house in the 1970s, the structure and garden stonework already in place directed the garden design. According to Green, the original garden was designed in the 1920s by William Monroe, Sr., who created the three terrace levels and the rock garden. The three levels are evidenced now as the upper parterre, the middle level pool, and the tennis court at the lower level. The rock garden directly in back of the house surrounds a stone terrace and is built upon the existing slope planted with hosta, sedum, liriope, ferns and azaleas. Swimming pool and statuary are placed on a direct axis with the den of the house, extending the terrace and serving as a garden focal point for that oft-used room. "It is a pattern reminiscent of Edwin Lu-

tyens' work at Hestercombe," Gainey points out. And to connect other elements of the house with further reaches of the garden, the paving stones leading from the back door are continued throughout the garden. One path leads to the parterre through what seem like low-lying clouds of white Annabelle hydrangeas and red leaf Japanese maples floating among the stout trunks of oak trees. Their foliage creates a striking chartreuse and crimson contrast in springtime. The same stonework is re-created at the entrance to the guest house, which has its own little section of garden. Another path, winding around the guest house to the opposite side of the house, fans out into a shallow, terraced descent to a quiet and secluded shady area, or "room." The casual ambler might not even notice the tennis court just steps away, accessible from the swimming pool area but not visible from the house or anywhere else in the garden. The garden's gentle hills and many levels not only enable convenient camouflage; they help to define its rooms and at the same time carry the feeling of one area flowing into another.

Stacked stone steps lead from the pool area to the parterre, which formerly was planted in hybrid tea roses. Stunning in effect but mind-boggling in maintenance, the formal rose garden is a fond memory preserved on these pages and has since been re-designed as a boxwood parterre. Inspired by Philip Shutze's work at the Patterson-Carr house in Atlanta, Gainey designed the fencing and gates enclosing what is now essentially a green and white garden. The surrounding border is of white hydrangeas, both Annabelle and Sister Theresa, white phlox, and lespedeza, also white—all of which bloom in succession from spring to summer. The focal point, a small water feature, fountain and trellis, also designed by Gainey, is entwined with a giant white clematis and sprinkled with the pale, soft petals of New Dawn roses.

The use of plant material is skillful and artistic, including some unusual plants. The blue evergreens in the shade garden, for example, are Boulevard cypress and *Cunninghamia lanceolata* 'Glauca,' which bring light to this part of the garden and contrast the double flowering salmon quince that is placed up high so its blooming under-branches can be appreciated. Also planted here are a yellow form of the native calycanthus, viburnums and cimicifuga. *Hydrangea arborescens grandiflora*, also called Hills of Snow, are planted in the front of the house, and recent additions are fastigiate gingkos and *Cornus alternifolia*, a dogwood whose branches grow in layers.

"All the elements of the garden, the trees, the plants, the architecture, the stonework, the treillage—all are part of the movement of the garden," says Gainey, "of walking through it, at every turn, at every arrival." Horticulturally, it continues to evolve, and certain plants are repeated throughout the garden to continue the flow, like the melodic theme of a symphony repeated in its various movements. It is as though this garden creates not only a sense of place, but a sense of journey and destination as well. As an artistic statement, as an aesthetic experience, it may never be finished, but it is complete. And the value of that is the satisfaction and sense of well-being it confers on those there to enjoy it.

Jackye Lanham and *Nawench*

$\mathcal{T}$his house speaks to me," Atlanta designer Jackye Lanham recalls telling her husband, Bill, on seeing the house for the first time. His response had to do with what, exactly, the house might be saying, venturing along the lines of "uh-oh." The house was due for a bit of refurbishing. But the designer was determined. "I didn't even know a house like this existed in Atlanta."

True, it is not the typical brick Georgian or clapboard colonial. But neither is Lanham a typical southerner. A self-proclaimed army brat, she grew up all over the country and traveled the world. Her mother was from Maine and

The Lanhams are avid readers, as their well-stocked library attests. A pillowed banquette beckons armchair globetrotters to see the world from a sunny bay window.
Opposite: The oval, marble foyer with its curving stair and striking, wrought iron banister makes a grand entry into the Lanham home, designed by Louisiana architect James Owen Southwell and built in 1925.

her father from Oregon. Perhaps the house spoke something of her heritage. Its shingle and stone construction would have been quite common in New England, and the hundreds of trees towering around it might evoke an Oregon landscape. Yet here it was in northwest Atlanta, and so was she. Built in 1925 by Felix DeGolian, the house is situated on a large and lushly wooded tract of land off Howell Mill Road. His son, Felix Jr., might have inherited the house, but he and his fourteen children wouldn't have fit. So he carved a road into the property (which has since been sub-divided) and built across the street, where he still lives today. His father named the original house *Nawench*, after the Polish clan from which he descended. The architect, James Owen Southwell, was from New Iberia, Louisiana, and at the time a professor at Georgia Tech. "But the house is crazy," Lanham beams, relishing its eccentricity. "All the angles and arches and levels. You almost get the feeling he did it tongue-in-cheek. And that is its charm. It begins with this very formal foyer and ends up being very cozy."

Departing the predictable, the freshness and simplicity of green and white toile give the Lanham dining room a different look.

Indeed, the oval entry with its marble floor, handsome architectural detail and curving stair with the unusual wrought iron banister has an air of grandness about it. "Yes, it is grand," Lanham admits, "but what I really like is that as you move through the house it becomes less and less so. If every room looked like the entrance hall, it would be too much, and pretentious, but this is just enough." To the right of the foyer, up one step, and through an arched, cased entry, is the living room. Straight ahead through the foyer is another step up into the hall, and the living and dining areas fan out from there. Surrounded by so many trees, it is not a sunny house, but it has a fresh, airy quality that is comforting. It has the soul of good design.

Forsaking fad and drama, Lanham begins by thinking about how she wants the finished room to look, how she wants it to feel, the colors she wants—and works backward from there. "I want everything to look natural and like it's supposed to be there, so when you walk in the room you don't say I love your curtains, or isn't that a pretty rug, or I love the fabric. I want you to walk in and just like it. And then your eye settles on one thing, and then another, and it's kind of fun." And she does like *things*—lots of them— though she avoids the chaotic appearance of over-accumulation.

Lanham avoids extensive use of color for herself (but not for her clients), opting for neutrals and simple chromatic schemes set off by strong contrasts, interesting textures and a diverse collection of art and objects.

"I like order and I like everything clean. I may have 25 things on a table, but it is orderly." In accessories and in furnishings, she juxtaposes formal and informal. "You want it to be serious, but not too serious, so you've gotta throw something in that shakes it down a little bit." For example, she has put sisal on the floor in the living and dining rooms, and has arranged her funky folk art pieces with fine period accessories. In the living room, an Edwardian bamboo chest is set with French bronze candlesticks, a *papier mâché* English sewing box, nineteenth-century brass ball buttons on a string, and "The Hand of God" by Ulysses Davis. A small, handlike sculpture painted gold and black and studded with pearls, the piece is kind of wild-looking, but elegant. "I guess that's what it is," Lanham says. "I like something that's elegant, but not a cliché."

Lanham is a connoisseur of contrasts. If it's white, she likes it with black

Top Left: In the downstairs powder room, a beautiful lavoratory is fashioned from an antique marble-topped console and accessorized with delicate candlestick lamps.

Top right: Antique baskets and gardening supplies are arranged haphazardly on an old butcher block table in an alcove off the kitchen. The ornamental wrought iron on the window is notable in other areas of the house as well.

Below: An unusual built-in basket system is topped by a marble counter, a pass-through from kitchen to breakfast room. Interior decorator Lanham designed the diagonal louvered doors for her cabinets. Above the counter is a small sample of a fine black and white Staffordshire dog collection.

Antique linen pillow shams are tacked to the windows of this sunny corner bath. The magnolias provide the privacy.

or mahogany. She pairs pale colors with deep, rich tones and textured neutrals. She avoids elaborate window treatments and fabrics that might weigh a room down. For instance, in her library, she says, "The books are so rich in their color that I like the contrast with pale beige toile, rather than, say, red, which would be abrupt to me. I like the combination of rich to pale." In her house with lots of windows and surrounded by green, Lanham has used a lot of white, wheat-colored sisal, blonde and dark woods, and dashes of color—green, of course, pale yellow, and spots of lavender and blue, which pick up the hundreds of hydrangeas that line the winding, uphill driveway and border the lawn. It is, as she has said, her letting the house and grounds dictate to her what is in sync and what is needed. And the house is lucky enough to have a designer who listens.

The Inman House in Buckhead

*S*ome houses, like some romances, are meant to be. In Buckhead, Suzanne and Edward Inman II have such a house, and the preeminent American architect, Charles W. Moore, designed it. Suzanne Inman had heard Moore speak at a seminar and later purchased a book that included one of his designs. As it turns out, it was The Design for her—an open floor plan built around a garden and courtyard. Moore, an American Institute of Architects gold medalist and professor of architecture at the University of Texas in Austin, got a call from the Inmans. Says Inman, "It all fell into place and it made more and more sense. Ed and I like contemporary architecture, and we like open spaces and a lot of light."

As if entering on aesthetic cue, Moore, who has been called "a grandfather of post-modernism," designed a house which not only esteemed symmetry in its contemporary form but incorporated neo-classical elements that referred to both the cultural and historical context of the South. The soaring, vaulted-ceiling foyer and triple-hung windows in the living and dining

rooms are gracious nods to the past expressed in modern terms, as are interior moldings, cornices, pilasters and capitals. The architectural detail was designed by Moore and executed by W. P. Stephens Lumber Co., the custom millwork business owned by Ed Inman. Also hailing from Inman's mill are the massive front doors. Mahogany with burled elm, they had been made for the Georgia Pacific boardroom and ultimately not used. When the Inmans took Moore to tour the mill, Ed pointed out the doors and suggested using them for the house. "And so the joke was that Charles scaled the house to those doors, and Ed teased that he would gladly have had them cut down."

And yet it is not a large house; it is rather a medium house that seems large. The bedrooms are small, the children's accommodating only a three-quarter bed or bunk beds, a small chest and a desk. The spaciousness of the public rooms is created as much by their high ceilings as by their square

Traditional, triple-hung windows flood the living room with light. The furniture is sculptural and covered in soft shades of silk. Molding and millwork in the architectural detail are exceptional throughout the house.

The soaring arch of the vaulted entry is echoed in the arches of the loggia, beyond. Tina Bebe consulted on paint colors to create a warm, atmospheric effect. The marble and gilt consoles once belonged to Ed's grandmother, Mrs. Edward H. Inman, who owned *Swan House*.

footage. "Charles is a very economical builder," Inman points out. "He interviews his clients extensively and then works within a budget to try to give them the elements and the image they want, without a great deal of cost." And indeed it is the Inmans' open floor plan which blurs the boundaries of the house and expands its limits. On either side of the foyer are the living and dining room, with the kitchen and breakfast room off the dining room. Two steps lead from the breakfast room to the hall, which curves around in a "C" and opens to each of the three children's rooms, to the master bedroom, and ends gracefully in an outdoor room or porch. In the middle is the courtyard, visible from nearly every vantage point in the house.

The interior decoration enhances the feeling of space and is imbued with a sort of elegant serenity, belying—or perhaps helping to balance—the active lives of the two adults and three young children within. Working with Tina Bebe, Inman avoided the cool, muted colors generally identified with post-modernism and chose rich, warm tones. Even the blue in the dining room is warm—atmospheric rather than icy. The same can be said of the sky-colored foyer ceiling and soft butterscotch walls. Furnishings, too, continue the architectural quality of the house and are large-scaled and sculptural. Living room sofas are upholstered in the palest, warm pink silk. The curtains, designed by Moore, are an over-scaled pastel silk plaid.

The look is clean and uncluttered but not cold. Judiciously selected accessories and family pieces personalize the house and make it "home." A pair of gilded console tables in the foyer once belonged to Mrs. Inman, Ed's great-grandmother, who built and lived in *Swan House*. Adorning their surfaces are crystallized ceramic vases collected by Suzanne. Antique, hand painted wallpaper panels are framed and installed in the dining room. The powder room vanity is a bookcase full of old, leather-bound volumes, its marble top set with beautiful antique silver pieces, perfume bottles and scented soaps. The hall holds a nineteenth-century secretary, an antique tapestry, and old family portraits.

When the house was completed in 1985, Moore described it drolly as "blown-out Georgian." Characteristically, there is a touch of whimsy in the Moore design as well. The *porte cochère* front entrance, for example, recalls a bygone era, when such *portes* were actually used by *cochères* and women wore skirts with hoops. Such elements may be Moore's architectural wink at old southern conventions and clichés, but not without the authentic ambivalence of a modern native. It is as if to say one should honor the importance of an aesthetic and a heritage, yet one shouldn't take it too seriously.

The South—the ante-bellum South in particular—evokes visions of classical and Georgian revival architecture, as in *Tara* and *Gone With the Wind*

The house has an open floor plan that encircles a garden and courtyard. This spring show of New Dawn roses is visible from nearly every part of the house.

The master bedroom is simple and elegant with its fine white linens, worn-soft silk upholstery, and ever-presence of nature through a wall of windows.

and so forth. And in Atlanta (where nearly none of that remains, thanks to a certain General Sherman), twentieth-century architects Neel Reid and Philip Shutze have left beautiful legacies in neo-classical, baroque and Renaissance revival forms, including the aforementioned *Swan House*, built by Ed Inman's late, great-grandparents, Mr. and Mrs. Edward H. Inman, in 1928. Nearly seventy years later, the young Inmans honor their southern heritage with a house which embodies a part of the past and builds upon it. "A choreography of the familiar and surprising" is successful architecture as defined by Moore. It is an apt metaphor for the Inman house, and perhaps, even for Atlanta itself—a city defined by its past and in some ways constrained by it, a city which, in its rise from the ashes, its civil rights struggles, its real estate booms and busts, and its hosting of the 1996 Olympic games, continues to surprise the world and sometimes itself with its ambition and achievement.

The Oriental Garden of Dorothy Fuqua

*I*n Atlanta, the name Fuqua brings to mind at least one extraordinary garden. The Dorothy Chapman Fuqua Conservatory at the Atlanta Botanical Garden is one of the city's treasures. Honoring his wife and her love of gardening, Atlanta businessman J.B. Fuqua donated funds for the building of a conservatory to be named for her. Since its completion in March of 1989, the Fuqua Conservatory has become home to the largest collection of coniferous plants and lithops in the country.

The "Japanesque" garden of Dorothy and J.B. Fuqua begins at the front door, where a small water feature and rock garden create a tranquil setting. Opposite: The view from the footbridge changes dramatically with the seasons. A few koi fish weave among the lily pads and papyrus. In June, the fabulous lotus grow to be five or six feet tall, with luminous pink blossoms as big as dinner plates.

But there is another extraordinary Fuqua garden in Atlanta. Slightly less exotic and most assuredly less public is Dorothy Fuqua's own garden at home. Marking the entrance is a graceful and weathered Japanese bamboo gate, surrounded by the foliage of magnolia, dogwood and azalea. In tufts and fronds at its base are grasses, ferns and nandina, punctuated by a small plaque on a low stake. Its inscription reads: *"If you'd have a mind at peace/A heart that cannot harden/Go find a door that opens wide/Upon a lovely garden."* And the landscape the little sign heralds is as lyrical as the verse. With a soothing rhythm, the garden's measures are ordered by a curving stone path, dotted and softened with mosses and ferns. It flows by a rhododendron grove, across a terraced area, winding gently uphill to a cedar and bamboo viewing house, Japanese stone lanterns, groups of plants and trees, and on through dry creek beds. Sloping back down behind the house and then curving back toward it, the path continues, arching into a redwood footbridge which leads again to the terrace. The bridge spans a small pond that is habitat to koi and magnificent summer-blooming lotus plants.

There are stunning views of the garden from the house, thanks to ample windows and sliding glass doors. Granddaughter Ruth Fuqua skips across the footbridge. Many of the ornamental plants now common in the United States originated in the Orient.

"Someone told me this was the most authentic Japanese garden he had seen in the United States," Mrs. Fuqua says "I had to tell him it was, in reality, 'Japanesque.'" Though the garden prospers by the stems and shoots of its Oriental counterparts—Japan and Georgia are on the same latitude—it also includes plants of the American South. Rather than be limited by difficult cultivars in the name of authenticity, Fuqua has begun to incorporate a variety of plants. "I don't fight nature," she says, "I just join it."

As a founding trustee of the National Wildflower Research Center in Austin, Texas, begun by her friend Lady Bird Johnson in 1972, Fuqua has an affinity for native plants. Interspersed along her garden path are Solomon's seal, wild ginger, crested iris, and ground cedar, all of which are native to Georgia. Forming a lush mat in another part of the garden is a native pachysandra, whose leaves are much larger than the Japanese version. Double orange daylilies and a running violet are two of the many plants Fuqua brought with her from her previous garden in Augusta, which she called "friendship garden" because so many plants in it were presents from friends. Sharing the bank are ferns, azaleas, hostas, pieris, bamboo, kerria (which was her grandmother's), helleborus and aucuba.

Covering the hills of the garden and framing the water feature and creek beds are plants chosen emphatically for their texture. In keeping with Japanese custom, combinations of azaleas, dwarf pines, spirea, dwarf lacy nandina, and blue rug junipers create rich textural effects. And as subtle texture is best appreciated at close range, so are other, more delicate elements of this environment. A miniature rock garden near the base of the footbridge is touched with the color of tiny violets and daisies, as well as bonsai elms, dogwoods, conifers, and azaleas that are but inches high, as if planted there by fairy gardeners.

It is this spirit of innocence, the simplicity and serenity of Japanese gardens that speak to Dorothy Fuqua and are, perhaps, antidotal. Before coming to Atlanta, the Fuquas lived in Augusta. In those days—from the late 1940s to 1967—her husband J.B. became a pivotal figure in Georgia politics and at the same time began building a company that would one day rank in the Fortune 500 and have its headquarters in Atlanta. To counter the hectic

Marigolds and begonias are great globes of color against the stones of the house and the bamboo towering above it.

Left: A bamboo gate at the side of the house marks the entrance to the garden, where a stone path leads the way.

Right: Hemlock and white-blooming mountain laurel shade a serene cedar and bamboo viewing house.

pace of an active corporate wife, Mrs. Fuqua began studying ikebana, the Japanese art of flower arranging, and her interest in Oriental gardens "just evolved," she says. It was just the kind of garden which pleased her most.

When the Fuquas moved to Atlanta they named their place on Tuxedo Road "Dogwood Hill," as it was dense with the native flowering tree. In her house, what began as a very contemporary decor was gradually infiltrated with Oriental pieces, from Japan and all over the Far East, before such eclecticism was fashionable. It seemed simply the thing to do, as the house's many large windows brought the garden into nearly every room. "There's something in bloom from February through December," Mrs. Fuqua adds. Earliest spring brings the bulbs peeking through with the late camellias. In May, the Siberian iris are splashes of yellow and white; the Japanese roof iris are a dramatic, blue-purple contrast. The dogwood and azaleas tint the spring from snowy-white to fiery crimson. And the luminous, porcelain pale pink of the lotus is a glorious gift of the summer. The maple, sourwood, dogwood and sassafras carry the fall, and the twilight of winter is brightened with berries and scented with daphne, grace notes at the end of the season and cues to return to the beginning.

Knox Clayton's House in Chastain

Clayton likes to collect things in groups, such as this growing set of yellow porcelains and pottery in the sitting room. **Opposite:** In the bedroom, yet another collection of glassware reflects its frosted colors in a mirrored table and picks up tones of the antique quilt.

One of the best things about summer in Atlanta is the open-air concerts at Chastain Park. Several times a week, from late spring to early fall, from classical to country to rock, the sounds of music come forth from the amphitheater that is very much a part of the north Atlanta neighborhood which claims it. During performances, audiences as diverse as the music itself munch picnic suppers and sip wine. Tables and trays are set with everything from silver candelabra and crudités to paper plates and buckets of chicken. The shows go on rain or shine and almost always end with a beautiful, flickering spectacle of tiny flames, as concert-goers hold candles, matches and lighters aloft in appreciation and appeal for an encore.

From where fashion and interior designer Knox Clayton listens a few blocks away, the music is somewhat faint, but he likes to think the good vibrations are felt throughout the neighborhood. "It's hard to believe Roswell Road is two blocks away, and here you're practically in the woods—it's like a jungle. I find that comforting—having the city and the jungle at the same time." But for Clayton, a Costa Rican native, the neighborhood was an afterthought. It was the house itself that won him.

He had seen it months before and knew it was the one he wanted. Not a bungalow and not a ranch, the house is pure 1946 modern, considered avant-garde for its time. Coincidentally, the house was built in the same year Clayton was born. "I definitely think it was karma. I was living in Midtown and a friend wanted me to see a house that was for sale on this street," Clayton begins. When he went to look he also strolled around the neighborhood and spied the house he now owns—which was not for sale. "And I thought if there's a house in Atlanta I would like to live in this would be it." A few months passed, and one day he just decided to ride by, just in case— and it was for sale.

The angular and somewhat austere exterior belies the spaciousness and light within. What began as a dim, boxy six rooms has been flung open, glassed in and aired out. The solid wooden front door was replaced with a three-paneled glass one. Pried away were the plywood panels above glass doors on the enclosed back porch to let more light in. Floor-to-ceiling French doors were installed between the living room and the porch, which also incorporates a dining area. Now the back yard is visible from the front door, lending an expansive feeling to the otherwise fairly small interior.

Sun pours through the large paneled windows and bounces off the white walls within. The floors are polished blond wood, and the fabrics—with the exception of those in the den—are for the most part in tones of beige and ivory. The effect is a subtle and quietly elegant light-and-shadow-box for

The "great room" at the back of the house combines living and dining areas and is Clayton's favorite for entertaining. White cotton canvas slipcovers club chairs and sofa. The coffee table is a rare, 18th-century Chinese piece in papier mâché.

rugs and textiles as brightly colored as tropical birds, and for collections ranging from African artifacts, to Art Deco accessories and objects, to pottery and art glass. Periods and cultures coalesce in unlikely but successful combinations, the sure mark of a man who knows what he likes and what his life is about. There's a certain emotional honesty in good eclectic decor, and Clayton has it.

His house reveals a man in harmony. The placement of such disparate art, objects and furniture, and their occasional rearrangement, is like a signature; not all the letters are alike or even formed in the same way, but the energy, the preferences and the personality that formed them are from a single source. The result is an artfully inscribed line that is not only unique but coherent, fluid, and deliberate. It is not necessarily legible, but that is not necessarily the point. Clayton's house, like the music from Chastain that pulses around it, has rhythm.

John Oetgen's House in Ansley Park

*T*t was big news in Atlanta when the Collier property came up for sale. George Washington Collier was one of Atlanta's original settlers and civic leaders, and the six hundred acres he had acquired just north of downtown was rightfully referred to as his "princely domain." As it remained unbreached during his lifetime, the land also became known as the "northside dam." Collier's death broke the dam, and when the property sold, *The Atlanta Journal* reported it was "by all odds the greatest real estate auction ever held in the South." Advertisement for the sale of one large parcel noted, "It is unnecessary to indulge in any word painting; the property speaks for itself and has been sought for many years." It went on magnanimously to include, "Ladies are particularly invited to attend . . ."

This two-hundred-and-two-acre lot bordered by Peachtree Street, Peachtree Circle, Montgomery Ferry Drive, Piedmont Avenue and Fifteenth Street was sold to Collier in 1847 for $150. When Collier died in 1903, the Southern Real Estate Improvement Company bought it the following year for $300,000 and recovered its entire purchase price from the re-sale of only about one-fourth of the property. Principals of the company included Edwin P. Ansley, who soon bought out his associates, and the development that began as Peachtree Garden became Ansley Park.

Ansley employed civil engineer Solon Z. Ruff, the same follower of Frederick Law Olmsted, Sr., who executed Olmsted's plan for Druid Hills. The Piedmont Avenue entrance to Ansley Park was designed to match that of Piedmont Park across the street, and the area is dotted with small parks throughout. Writing in the second volume of *Atlanta and Environs*, historian Franklin Garrett remarked that "substantial Atlantans" built homes in Ansley, and, "for the most part they are still owned by good citizens, and

Ansley Park remains today probably the best 'close-in' residential section of Atlanta."

John Oetgen's Queen Anne-style brick house on Peachtree Circle was built around 1910 and lived in by the city's most sought after milliner. "Everyone came here for their hats," Oetgen says. Several owners and a duplex division later, the house is again inhabited by one of the city's premier creative spirits. A popular and oft-published interior designer, Oetgen manages an impressive client list, owns an antiques business, and lends his time and talent to a number of charity events. He also paints and draws. So

The "garden room" in reality overlooks a parking lot, though clever use of trellis and plants might convince otherwise. A blue ceiling gives depth and coolness, and antique pediments are shelves for favorite things.

A subtle silk stripe on the chair, mossy velvet on the banquette and smooth leather on the ottoman contrast with the nubby texture of the seagrass floorcovering. Cream-colored walls are painted with swirling eternity symbols and adorned with gilded plaster moons and stars.

Light streaks across an Art Deco commode in the living room. Floor-to-ceiling curtains hang from steel pipes and emphasize the room's lovely proportions.

it follows that his work is not only multi-faceted but marked by an artful and sometimes playful quality. With touches of whimsy and special effects ranging from the theatrical to the mysterious, this designer's house could be the habitat of a sophisticated harlequin, an analogy Oetgen himself evokes. While he is certainly serious about design, he doesn't want the design to appear to take itself too seriously. So Oetgen's work always lightens up at just the right moment.

In what he calls the garden room, two antique pediments form shelves which are filled with objects that have nothing to do with each other except that they are some of Oetgen's favorite things. The dining room, with its shimmering stripes of blue and green and dots of light dancing on the ceiling, could be underwater stage scenery. Slightly more conventional, but no more predictable, is the living room, reminiscent of a European salon whose purpose lends itself to a lively exchange of ideas and the latest gossip. Mossy velvet covers the French-inspired banquette and slipper chairs, which can be readily rearranged to accommodate conversation. Warm beige walls are highlighted with the harlequin's touch—gilded plaster stars, half-moons, and the swirling symbols for eternity. A harlequin statue—Oetgen's muse?—stands atop a coffee table. A faintly post-modern feel is balanced nicely by fine antiques, which Oetgen loves. "Each piece is handmade and has its own history, so it doesn't belong to us really—we just own the right to enjoy it while we're here." Antiques, too, are symbols for eternity.

Upstairs, in the studio and sitting room Oetgen has painted a riotous mural: Henri Rousseau gone red, orange and wild, depicting scenes of places he loves to travel—Tuscany, the French Riviera village of Eze (on the Grand Corniche), and Guadeloupe. Crimson upholstery is piled with pillows and accented with a bold black and white print. At the opposite end of the hall, countering all that clamor, is the bedroom. In calming, soft shades of white with pale, clear blue at the windows, the room is elegantly simple. Minimalist in its unfussy window treatments, unadorned iron bed and "First" chair by Ettore Sottsass, the room avoids clutter but sacrifices no comfort.

Oetgen grew up in Atlanta and New York, graduated in design from Georgia State, and chose to remain in Atlanta. He is intent now on staying

In the foyer of his Ansley Park duplex, John Oetgen plants a hall tree in the form of a faux column stuck with gold-painted spikes. Grossgrain ribbon trim is affixed with thumbtacks.

A collection of prints, photographs and books are decoration enough for this bedroom that avoids starkness by the luxury of its French *La Nuit* linens, also apparently enjoyed by "Cody," the decorator's dog.

in Ansley Park. "I love the sidewalks and the trees and the parks, which virtually go end to end. There are wide boulevards, interesting architecture and a diverse group of people living here—some of the stars of the city." There are prominent old-line Atlantans, artists, politicians, socialites and certifiably eccentric characters. Of course, occasionally the categories overlap, and many know one another and speak on their afternoon strolls. "There's a real sense of community here," Oetgen says, "and that's increasingly rare these days. I wouldn't live anywhere else."

The Weber Garden on Park Lane

*B*efore it became Ansley park, the sprawling and sylvan Midtown neighborhood was farm land belonging to the Collier family, who, in 1822, descended from the hills of Gwinnett County to be among the city's earliest and most prominent white pioneers. One of fifteen children, George Washington Collier—"Wash," they called him—was a young boy then, but he must have shared his parents' vision of the potential this nascent Georgia settlement had. Wash grew up to be a major landholder, civic leader and the city's first postmaster, discharging his duties from his combined grocery store and post office at Five Points, downtown. The house he lived and died in, built by his father in 1823, is the oldest surviving in Atlanta and stands, albeit extensively renovated, in a development called Sherwood Forest, directly north of Ansley Park.

Also still standing is the house Wash's nephew, Henry L. Collier, built (circa 1920) in what is now Ansley Park. But unlike the house of his famous

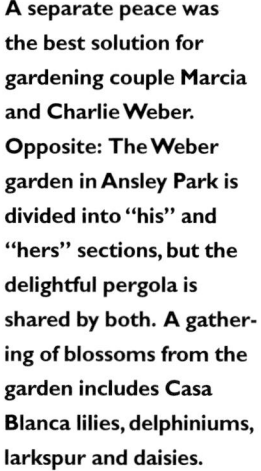

A separate peace was the best solution for gardening couple Marcia and Charlie Weber. Opposite: The Weber garden in Ansley Park is divided into "his" and "hers" sections, but the delightful pergola is shared by both. A gathering of blossoms from the garden includes Casa Blanca lilies, delphiniums, larkspur and daisies.

forebear, indeed unlike most of Atlanta, the house on Park Lane looks today much as it did then. "We're only the third owners," notes current resident Charlie Weber, "which is why nothing's ever been done to it. It's never even been air-conditioned." The second owner was landscape architect and orchid enthusiast Jim Wallace, who worked with Weber and his wife Marcia at the same landscape contracting firm. Every now and then when the Webers would see Jim at work, he would tell them, "You know, y'all need to buy my house." And, eventually, the Webers thought so, too.

Jim retired and moved out of the house. The Webers moved in, inheriting not quite a garden, but some garden houses—a row of three, aging and steam-heated, standing vigil down one side of the fifty-by-three-hundred-foot-long sliver of back yard. That left them with about half a sliver on which to garden—together. Opinions clashed and tempers flared. The Weber garden became fertile ground for connubial conflict. "I mean, we'd go three days not speaking over pruning *one limb,*" Marcia says. So, out came the greenhouses, save one, and in came the Webers' new creed: united they stand; divided they garden. The line, so to speak, was drawn in the form of a neat evergreen hedge right down the middle. Never was a war of the roses so amicably resolved. It wasn't just about roses, of course. The conflict had spread to nearly every blade, branch and flower. The solution was His and Hers. And hands off.

Aside from its purpose as peacekeeper, the hedge (*Thuja occidentalis* 'American Emerald Green') divides the garden into two rooms, so the entire garden is not seen at once, as Marcia says. "And you have a little surprise." Via the shaded stone terrace at the end of the garden nearest the house is the entrance to Charlie's side. It is a neatly trimmed strip of grass bordered by plantings in green and white, stachys, white impatiens and Candidum caladiums, with a touch of blue hydrangea. Like the fictional ideal child, it is quiet and orderly. Also, his side's slightly lower maintenance requirement left time to pursue his former passion of racing vintage sports cars. Now that he's recently given up that particular hobby, perhaps new things bode in his garden. For Charlie, in gardening and presumably in automobiles, the design's the thing.

The cutting shed is command central for the Webers' commercial florist business. It is a picturesque setting for an office, complete with birds' nests and resident winged friends.

For Marcia, it is the process and the experimenting; plants for plants' sake. Charlie (rhymes with jolly, as Marcia pronounces it) calls it her "stamp collection." Marcia says her husband is slightly smug about his restrained and understated landscape—"It isn't all muddled up like mine." But what a magnificent muddle it is—of lilies, modern hybrid tea and old roses, and adventurous color combinations such as lime green coleus, *Coreopsis verticillata* 'Moonbeam', and melampodium.

The garden, both sides, is also a laboratory for the couple's garden design and commercial florist business, now in its second decade. And the garden thrives, relieved, perhaps, from the stress of its caretakers' squabbles. One musn't argue in front of the garden, dear.

80

Bill Cook and Jay Reynolds on The Prado

Bill Cook barred no holds in his upstairs sitting room. Flying colors are grounded by comfortable, large-scaled furniture and floor cushions.

*W*ith elevations close to 1,000 feet in some places, Ansley Park was designed to follow gracefully the sway of the piedmont. And lovely though it may be, as Franklin Garrett points out in his *Atlanta and Environs*, it is also "an easy place in which to get lost, owing to the irregularity of the streets." But eventually one stumbles onto either Peachtree or Piedmont, from which it seems all in-town destinations are navigable. Ansley Park, begun in 1904, is designated in the National Register of Historic Places as "Atlanta's first automobile suburb." So important were the new-fangled motor cars' pathways that developer Edwin P. Ansley held a contest to name them. La Fayette Drive, Westminster Drive and The Prater were among the winners. The Prater was reportedly named after the famous Viennese park, but it was later changed to The Prado. Today, The Prado is a popular and scenic route by which to wind one's way through Ansley Park from Peachtree to Piedmont, arriving near the Atlanta Botanical Garden and the Piedmont Driving Club, adjacent to Piedmont Park.

The Prado is also the address of Bill Cook and Jay Reynolds, whose 1905 house was one of the first built in Ansley. Cook calls the architecture Pennsylvania Dutch colonial, though it is a designation he adheres to but momentarily. The exterior—with its cottage-style landscaping and blooming windowboxes—honors its past well enough, as does the entrance porch, which Cook says is "really an outdoor room." Here, floral chintzes are mixed with kitchen-towel plaids, old wicker, French bistro chairs and hooked rugs. A few pieces of Majolica are tacked to the wall along with a plastic owl, the kind gardeners set out to scare off critters. "Nothing is fine; everything has a little bit of wear on it," Cook says, but it conveys a charm and unpretentiousness appropriate to the house. Beyond that room, how-

ever, anything goes—and does. Each room is wildly different. One or two are wild, period. And yet they work together, to each its own.

In the foyer, pale yellow walls serve as backdrop for a collection of black and white photographs, an art deco bench and plant stand, and a sleek, sheer window treatment. On the powder room door is painted a *trompe l'oiel* blackamoor holding a tray of tequila and lemons. The ersatz host merely hints that the further you go, the less there is what you'd expect. The neutral-toned living room is classic Anglo-colonial, with European and

A bedroom in black, white and Deco is masculine and comfortable. The Charles Eames "Low Rider" chair is a snazzy newsstand.

A glass block wall and Matisse-inspired Prismater fabric on a banquette give the breakfast area in the kitchen a souped-up Caribbean flavor.

Oriental touches. Low-voltage halogen lighting supplies a subtle but extremely important dimension to the look of the room. Since the room is for visiting and entertaining, the furniture and objects are quiet, so as not to compete with the company and conversation. By contrast, the dining room with its dark, glossy colors, heavy fabrics and stage-set *trompe l'oiel* fireplace is bold, showy and dramatic. Upstairs, the master bedroom is calming and slightly surreal in black and white toile, and cool with its Ruhlman-inspired chest and Corbusier lounge. The guest room comes straight from Grandma's, with Victorian antiques and fluff. Just footsteps away is a zoom through the centuries: Duncan Phyfe meets the Jetsons—with neo-Regency motifs, Deco shapes and space-age bright colors.

These apparent decorative opposites are partly explained by the personalities inspiring them. Cook is an interior designer, and Reynolds designs women's party clothes with a flair for the splashy and fun. Cook says incorporating his housemate's tastes has challenged him as a designer and struck a balance in the process. In the kitchen, Cook wanted country French, and Reynolds wanted high-tech. They compromised with a sort of souped-up Caribbean look, softened with butcher block countertops and shined up with a commercial stainless steel gas range. The kitchen and breakfast room are the one area where a previous owner made structural changes in the otherwise un-changed house, adding a sunny, soaring breakfast room with a wet bar and fireplace. Outside, the pair has created another outdoor room on the terrace, where a Carolina jessamine-covered treillage shelters a many-pillowed settee. Pots of geraniums bloom all summer long, and a narrow allée beside the house has been transformed into a formal rose garden with a herringboned brick walkway.

It's as though the house is a cycle through time: early twentieth century from exterior to entrance, progressing through decades and several decorative periods inside, then emerging through the back terrace again into a more traditional southern motif but with a bright updated look in fabrics and colors. The house is comfortable in past, present and future—perhaps a hopeful metaphor for the city itself. With places, as with people, appearances can deceive.

84

The Midtown Apartment of Timothy Tew

*T*t is appropriate that the home of Timothy Tew, one of Atlanta's leading young art dealers, was built during an important period in the city's early cultural development—and in the same Midtown neighborhood. In 1903, at a home on Fourteenth Street—just blocks away from Tew's on Myrtle Street—there was a fortuitous meeting of art lovers which led to the chartering of the Atlanta Art Association. Then, in 1926, Mrs. Joseph Madison High, widow of a prominent Atlanta merchant, gave her house to the Association to be used as an art museum. It is on and around that site on Peachtree Street just north of Fifteenth that the Robert W. Woodruff Memorial Arts Center thrives today, comprising not only the High Museum of Art but Symphony Hall, the Atlanta College of Art and the Alliance Theatre.

Although Galerie Timothy Tew is located on Bennett Street, the eclectic

On a shady side street in Midtown, Tew's apartment occupies part of the second floor of this capacious clapboard mansion built in the early 20th century.
Opposite: A 1950s desk in a corner of the bedroom anchors works (clockwise from bottom left) by Stewart Helm, a pair of Marie Cécile-Aptel scarabs flanking an oil by Jean de Beton, and a portrait of Stewart Helm by Haidee Becker.

district of galleries, antique shops and what-nots off Peachtree Street in Buckhead, Tew prefers to live in the more urban, less mainstream atmosphere of Midtown, several miles south. A relative rarity vis-à-vis modern Atlanta suburbia, Tew's is an old-fashioned neighborhood of rambling, clapboard, early twentieth-century houses, great old trees and wide sidewalks. His house was built between 1910 and 1915, and, like others on the street, has long since been converted to apartments. He says that his second-

A delicate Directoire chandelier casts soft light on works (clockwise from bottom left) by Charles Keiger, Isabelle Melchior, Aujame, Stewart Helm, Melchior, Lucy Currie and Paul Morn.

floor flat gives him the feeling of a tree house, which, while admittedly small with three rooms and a kitchen, is by no means creatively confining. The collector within has been unafraid to branch out among the best new artistic talent he could find, both here and abroad.

Tew approaches his rooms as galleries. The furnishings are simple and uncluttered, with spare lines and little ornamentation. "My friends accuse me of being stuck in the fifties, and I'm not," he says. "But there is a certain aesthetic about it I like. America was at its height then." Perhaps by karmic coincidence, Tew's neighborhood was a run-down residential area which was revived in the late 1950s, thanks to the venerable Atlanta architect and urban pioneer Henri Jova leading the way at Mentelle Drive and Seventh Street. The same decade also corresponds to the artists whose work Tew

Gallery owner Tew surrounded by works, clockwise from top left, by Isabelle Melchior, Haidee Becker, Edith Ainsworth, Cérore (the pair of yellow and red figure studies), a poem painted on a mirror by Peg Morar, and a tree painting by Charles Keiger. The colorful, carved wood sculpture is by Kimo Minton.

In the tiny kitchen a zany exhibit of "I Love Lucy" plates and 1950s appliances lend a fun, quirky note to the owner's collection, which, not accidentally, is partly of the same era.

collects and represents. They range from those who, like Tew, were born in the fifties, to those who were schooled in the traditional disciplines of drawing and painting in the forties and fifties.

From hand-me-downs, flea markets and a few choice purchases like the John Dickinson leather sofa in the living room, Tew has created the look of a slightly Bohemian European salon, where the art and furniture have been together long enough to seem like old friends—if not yet companions through the generations, then soul mates. In Tew's bedroom, a cubist figural composition and a haunting portrait work well with a contemporary still life and a pair of unusual tempera paintings of giant scarabs, all hanging together above the sleek, black Paul McCobb desk and the ridiculous "Southern belle" ceramic lamps with mismatching shades. The dining room, with its handsome glass-topped table, Biedermeier chairs, and floor-to-ceiling beautiful art, segues into the kitchen, which sports a wacky collection of commemorative *I Love Lucy* plates and period small appliances. "They still work!" he exclaims gleefully. Arguably like all good contemporary artists and their patrons, Tew may have a touch of the iconoclast in his aesthetic inclinations.

In decorating, he has worked with what he was given, acquired what he could afford, and been sensitive to where and how he has lived, from the rural American South to cosmopolitan Europe. Tew is a Georgia native who studied for a year in Paris at the Sorbonne and in a private school for dealers in art and antiques. "The South gave me an appreciation for gentility and for beautiful things. There is a certain aesthetic here, and an appreciation for tradition, that I respect without being restricted by. And then living in Paris influenced me a great deal," Tew says. "The French just seem to live with things more as they are—their furniture, their art, their draperies—maybe because so much more is handed down. It just showed me how nice worn-out things could be. They aren't constantly trying to make rooms look new." Furniture and objects take on the unmistakable patina of the passing of time, and there is no reproducing it. Taking a cue from the Europeans, Tew also is content to live with what he has, let the newness wear off, and see the beauty and style endure.

John Howard and Benjamin Roden-Lupton in Palmer House

In the entrance, a limestone block console with cast iron legs is the work of artist Marshall Davis.

Opposite: Furnished with one-of-a-kind art pieces and funky vintage finds, the Howard/Roden-Lupton residence has the dazzling Midtown skyline on permanent exhibit. The marble coffee table was designed and fabricated by Howard.

*S*ave for the odd patch of grass or tree-planted sidewalk, the nearest thing to a landscape is blocks away. Nevertheless, a couple of landscape architects have an unshakeable preference for Midtown. Though not officially designated as such until the early 1970s, Midtown is more or less the area between Buckhead and downtown, including Piedmont Park and the neighborhood of Ansley Park. "We think it's the best part of the city," says John Howard; and his partner, Benjamin Roden-Lupton, agrees. "Everything we do is in this part of town." Their office is seven blocks away. The arts venues are here; Piedmont Park is a short walk; and the airport is a twenty-minute MARTA ride.

Benjamin and John live in Palmer House, a Neel Reid-designed apartment building constructed in 1908, on Peachtree Place, off Peachtree Street just south of Tenth. The neighborhood in the old days was almost all residential. Today it is towers of granite and glass, with the occasional older building, small restaurant or shop. There is also one other notable holdout: on the corner of Peachtree and Tenth is the house where Margaret Mitchell once lived, and where she wrote *Gone With the Wind*. It was a hard-fought battle to save the abandoned, falling-down house which Mitchell herself called "the dump." Distinguished more for its famous tenant than for its architecture or aesthetic appeal, the house is now in the planning stages of restoration. Its advocates hope the house will one day be a museum and attraction for tourists who, dissappointed to learn there is no actual *Tara*, will be able to see the next best thing.

And Howard and Roden-Lupton can take it all in from their living room window. It is a remarkable view in more ways than one. There, on a flat, grassy lot, is "the dump," a piece of Atlanta history and reminder of both an era and a frame of reference, a legacy that is both proud and painful. As

if to overcome and atone, the brazen and beautiful Midtown skyline rises in the distance beyond, and Howard and Roden-Lupton enjoy its show of lights each twilight. At least half the buildings have been built in the six or so years he's lived here, Howard says, although, unfortunately, he's seen as many demolished.

The view inside the Howard-Roden-Lupton residence is also changing, as the budget permits and the two young collectors themselves grow and change. The apartment has good "bones"—large rooms, high ceilings, lots of windows, and gleaming floors. The absence of rugs creates a sense of coolness and space, conferring emphasis on the architecture. A spare and clean look is sculpted softly by well-placed track lighting. The focused beam on a bouquet of dill on the coffee table gives the simple arrangement another dimension and gracefully centers the room. The mostly twentieth-century furnishings are from funky vintage furniture shops and galleries, highlighted by the Patrick Nagar winged, black lacquer "Hell's Angel" chair in the living room and the Marshall Davis limestone block console table with cast-iron legs in the foyer. John designs furniture as well, and fabricates it himself. The rough-hewn, layered marble coffee table and the small, painted wooden cabinet in the living room are samples of his work. A pair of 1950s club chairs in their original sunflower-yellow synthetic are set off by the Hell's Angel and a dalmation-print Barcelona-style chair to form a comfortable seating area around the fireplace. The paintings are bold and contemporary, and highly stylized.

Elsewhere, the art and furniture which may not qualifiy as "permanent collection," as Roden-Lupton says, meanwhile are innovative and fun—although the team who manhandled the solid concrete dining set all the way to the fifth floor might argue with the "fun" part. Details like the fern fronds in bud vases on the lavatory belie the style and resourcefulness of these two, as do the potted plantings on their terraces. The small, back terrace they have transformed into a lush oasis of foliage and flowers that might be the romantic balcony of an Italian palazzo. The red-tiled roofscape visible from there and from the left-bare dining room windows reinforces the image. "It does give you the feel of being in Europe," says Roden-Lupton. "That's one of the things about this apartment," Howard says. "When you're in it, you could be anywhere in the world."

In the hands of two talented young garden designers, what might have been a dingy back stair is transformed into a lush terrace garden.

Laura Turner Seydel's Midtown Pied-à-Terre

*T*t probably isn't easy being the daughter of Ted Turner, but Laura Turner Seydel seems to be managing well enough. The brash and brilliant man who built a media empire from a billboard company, won the America's Cup twice, and married movie star Jane Fonda, casts a fairly long shadow in this town. And yet Laura does not rest in its shade. She wanted to own her own business, and the Buckhead clothing boutique, Sasha Frisson, is it. "I could have worked for CNN in New York, or done something like that, but I wanted to live in Atlanta," she says. "I have a lifetime of family and friends here, and I feel Atlanta is coming into its own. It's fun to watch a city advance culturally and to be a part of it." She is also active in community affairs.

That Laura is independent and confident of her own identity is quite stunningly manifested in her former Midtown high-rise condominium. Designed by Bill Cook, this pied-à-terre on three levels makes a bold statement in art deco and Russian empire, rich jewel tones, gilded accessories and luxe faux finishes.

The foyer, though tiny, fulfills its purpose grandly in providing transition from the mundane institutional hallway outside to the dramatic and highly stylized spaces inside. Its dark, glossy walls, pin-lights and high-contrast compass rose floor invite the eye to glide from there to the main salon with its slick blond wood floors, cream-colored walls, and soaring ceiling. Faux gemstones are sewn as if sprinkled over the the floor-to-ceiling curtains which span the width of the room and shimmer in an iridescent sapphire, like an evening dress. It is a nighttime space, evoking images of satin and marabou-clad starlets and dashing wax-haired dancing men. The black lacquer Russian empire dining table and console glimmer in the lights of the skyline. Even the kitchen—in polished granite and sleek stainless steel—is glamorous.

The two-story-tall window affords a sweeping view of the treetops of Piedmont Park and the downtown skyline. Sleek Art Deco furnishings in opulent fabrics gleam in the twilight. Of particular interest are a 1950s cone-shaped tortoise shell lamp and the semainier by Reid Leonard of Atlanta's IBM tower in Midtown.

Russian Empire reigns in the dining room. Cook's striking diamond-pattern design for the curtains derives from the table inlay, which he also designed.

A spiral staircase ascends to the master suite, where romance and neo-classicism make fine bedfellows—with a few funky touches, such as the pair of grand antique Meissen urns on the mantel illumined by a brushed steel standing candelabrum. Or the low wall of glass block forming a balcony overlooking the living room. Or the antique tapestry pillows softening an iron bed dressed in hard-edged black and white. The mural, painted on a curving wall, echoes an Italian landscape, the warm, muted colors of which are reflected in the Aubusson-style needlepoint rug. The dressing room and bath are pure, gilded Hollywood—crimson damask and gold brocade, tassels and trims, and the smoothest black marble. The closet, with its tiger-striped carpet and leopard settee, is smoldering. "When I first began working on this apartment," Cook recalls, "I wanted people standing outside on the sidewalk to look up here and think, 'What hot babe lives up there?' I mean I think this is a really bitchy apartment—very vamp.

"At least it started out to be very vampish," Cook checks himself. Things have changed a bit since then. The "hot babe" is now the wife of Rutherford Seydel and the mother of Rutherford III. A change in lifestyle will inevitably accompany a change in sensibilities, aesthetic and otherwise. When people's lives change, their homes change with them. Since the birth of their child, the Seydels have moved from the Midtown apartment into a house perhaps more suitable to the needs of a young, growing family. Fortuitously, Bill Cook and Laura Turner Seydel started with classic, if not necessarily traditional, styles, and they have worked with new, modern pieces as well as inherited old ones. The new house is—well, yes—more traditional, says Seydel, more English in feeling. And yet, she says, "We are using every piece from the apartment, even the Deco things—though they don't look quite as Deco when they're spread out and not all together in one or two rooms." The basics, when they are good, are unerringly adaptable. And *voilà:* hot babe becomes cool mom, with a house that says so—and celebrates it.

Design imitates life, as it should. At a personal level, it also tells a story—of progress, of maturing, of sureness in one's identity and one's place in the stages of life. So far for the Seydels, a good beginning, a happy ending.

Wade Burns's Garden in West End

**Burns pauses on a bench in his "outdoor room." Lushly carpeted with grass and walled with Leyland cypress, it has been the site of many a lawn game and good time.
Opposite: A blue juniper topiary is underplanted with blue fescue and bejeweled with a pink mandevilla. A cloud of coreopsis hovers below.**

Atlanta architect Wade Burns may be a Johnny-come-lately to gardening, but he is no neophyte in the area of high hopes—one of the gardener's most important prerequisites. In 1969, fresh from the school of architecture at Virginia Tech, the North Carolina native and preacher's son arrived in Atlanta. Whatever faith might have been passed on from father to son was called upon mightily, as a determined young man set out to lead the revival of a neighborhood. "There is an awful lot of faith involved," he told a newspaper reporter back then. "Sometimes you just feel that something is right."

Heaven knows it didn't start out that way. The story of the southwest Atlanta neighborhood called West End is an all-too-familiar story of cities across America: an affluent nineteenth-century suburb becomes a poor, twentieth-century inner city. West End grew from a settlement around White Hall Tavern, which once stood at the corner of present-day Gordon and Lee streets. The city's most prominent families lived there, and Atlanta's first suburb was considered quite grand. One famous son is Joel Chandler Harris, for years the highly popular humorist and editorial photographer for the *The Atlanta Constitution*, but best known to the world as the creator of Uncle Remus, Br'er Rabbit and company. Harris's home, restored and open year-round for tours and other activities, is at Ralph David Abernathy Drive and Lawton Street.

As Burns recounts it, West End prospered and grew through the 1890s, when people began moving to Inman Park, and, in the decade following, to Ansley Park. In the 1920s, some who remained began building small houses in Morningside. They lived there, closer to town, during the week, maintaining their West End homes for weekends and holidays. When the Depression hit, they kept the little houses and left the big ones. By the time World

War II came, many of the houses had been divided into apartments, and the neighborhood was failing.

But West End never lost its charm. In 1970, Burns bought a rambling, clapboard mansion built in 1856—purportedly the second oldest house in the city—and began to renovate. A few years later, marshalling a full force of workers and funds raised from public and private sources, Burns bought twenty-four houses in a block and went to work.

The houses sold, and gradually, a middle class—both black and white—re-established itself. The neighborhood had been integrated from the beginning, when the people who lived in the mansions had a lot of help taking care of them, and the help lived in humbler dwellings nearby. Today, nearly twenty years later, there is still a ways to go. There is a need for more businesses, more residents, a stronger tax base. But the sense of community has been restored. With that tangible, bricks-and-mortar commitment, says Burns, there was a halo effect among the residents. "There was a revival of spirit, and there was hope."

And as for Burns, he finally found time for himself and his garden, which he readily admits is beyond his "urban crisis architecture" area of expertise. But with the help of his friends and horticultural mentors Billie and John Elsley (he is the noted English horticulturist and director of horticulture for Wayside Gardens in Greenwood, South Carolina), Burns has persevered. His garden is interesting and diverse, but at the same time relatively uncomplicated and easy to maintain. It comprises essentially three elements: a shade garden in the front; a sunny swimming pool area in the back; and, to the side, an extraordinary "outdoor room" of classical European design.

In front of the house, beneath a canopy of giant white oaks, the delicate fronds of Christmas fern meander in and among the large, fan-like leaves of 'Sum and Substance' hosta. Vinca minor covers the ground, and Solomon's Seal and epimedium form borders. What color there is, is quiet, in keeping with the tone of the garden. There are the pinks and mauves of helleborus and the whites and wines of astilbe. Kousa dogwoods, anise, and a white Japanese maple have been planted as understory.

To the back of the house, the cool, muted palette turns warm and bright. A swimming pool and considerable paved surface dominate, but not at the

Rudbeckia Goldsturm, crape myrtle and miscanthus border a parking area between the pool, garage and studio, and the "outdoor room."

Wade Burns's West End house is one of the oldest in the city. A shady front yard, dominated by giant white oaks, is planted with Christmas ferns and Sum and Substance hosta.

expense of the garden. "The number one thing the Elsleys have taught me is subtlety in color and texture," Burns explains. "Back here there are strong colors, but there are no harsh combinations. There is a nice mix of burgundy and yellow and green." The *Rudbeckia* 'Goldsturm' interplanted with ornamental grasses and Russian sage is particularly striking. From there the eye travels upward, where planters on the balcony of the pool house and studio spill over with white petunias and ivy-leafed geraniums. White crape myrtles grow on either side of a statue by the pool, and pots set about the deck are bright with sun-loving annuals.

The tremendous rectangular outdoor room occupies an adjacent lot. Planted with grass and enclosed by Leyland cypress and cryptomeria, this elegant, verdant courtyard is a lovely setting for an afternoon of croquet or a twilight of solitude. It is a place where Burns might contemplate the paradox of this pastoral setting in its ultra-urban environment, and where he might take time to appreciate his worthy accomplishment in leading the restoration of this neighborhood.

Reynolds Cottage at Spelman College

One Sunday morning in 1883, from the pulpit of a church in Cleveland, Ohio, two young white women—Baptist missionaries and former abolitionists—made a plea for the funding of a school in Atlanta for the education of freed women slaves. A man from the congregation approached them afterwards: "Will you stick?" he asked them. "Of course we will," they said, and he emptied his pockets on the spot and gave them what he had—two hundred dollars or so. "And I will help you more," he said. And he did.

The man was John D. Rockefeller. The women were Harriet Giles and Sophia Packard. And the school that began as Atlanta Baptist Female Seminary in the basement of the Friendship Baptist Church is known today in

In the "Africa room," casual furnishings and neutral fabrics are accented with African textiles. The scheme makes a good setting for African and Caribbean artworks belonging to Dr. Cole and her family. Opposite: Assembled during her work as an anthropologist, Dr. Cole's collection of African objects fills a bookshelf and makes a fine exhibit.

southeast Atlanta as Spelman College. In response to Rockefeller's largess, the school was re-named for his mother-in-law Lucy Henry Spelman, herself a dedicated abolitionist. A century later, the small, all-female liberal arts college, with its enrollment of more than 2,000, has been cited by *U.S. News & World Report* as the number one regional, liberal arts college in the southeast, the only black college ever to be rated as number one.

Along with Morehouse College, Morehouse School of Medicine, Clark Atlanta University, Interdenominational Theological Center, and Morris Brown College, Spelman is part of the Atlanta University Center, an alliance unique in the world. "It may well be the largest coming together of African-American students in the world," says Spelman President Johnnetta Cole. "One has to say it just belongs in Atlanta. It belongs in Atlanta because Martin Luther King, Jr., went to Morehouse, because Marian Wright Edelman is a graduate of Spelman, and because of a new generation of the Spike Lees and the A. J. Johnsons (graduates of Morehouse and Spelman, respectively). There's clearly a set of reasons historically why these institutions

In the shade of a great, spreading oak stands Reynolds Cottage, named for Mary C. Reynolds, corresponding secretary of the Women's Baptist Mission Society. It was built at the turn of the century as the official residence of the president of Spelman College.

began here, but now you could not rip, tear or exorcise these institutions out of the Atlanta fabric."

Since coming to Spelman in 1987, Dr. Cole has woven her own fabric of professional obligations, civic duty, and home and family life—the threads of which are woven tightly together. It is less than a minute's walk from the front door of her office to the back door of her house, and she confesses a slight envy for those who manage a separation between work and home. "I try not to see home as an extension of the office," she begins, "but I cannot cease to see it as the official residence of the president of Spelman College. How I try to counteract some of that feeling is to mix things—furniture, art—that belong to my family with the things that belong to the college. For instance, in what we call the 'Africa room,' all the art belongs to me and my family, largely pieces I collected as an anthropologist. The furniture belongs to Spelman."

Talk of the meaning of home, of shelter, evokes in Dr. Cole her academic roots in anthropology. A Florida native and mother of three, Dr. Cole earned her master's and doctorate in anthropology at Northwestern University and was a professor at Hunter College and the City University of New York before coming to Spelman. "In the dining room," she continues, "that is my mother's dining room set, but the art on the walls belongs to the college. That kind of melding makes me feel at home here." Her havens in the house are her spacious bedroom upstairs and the screened-in porch off the living room downstairs. Even though the porch looks out over the campus, she says, "It gives me a wonderful feeling of comfort and contentment, so that is where I go to center myself."

Reynolds Cottage is a twenty-seven-room Victorian frame house built at the turn of the century. "And I must be very honest; the house needs a lot of work and is begging for us to find the resources to make it all that it can be." But the pragmatist in her concedes, "Well, part of what that does is it lets you relax in a house. It is a house we respect profoundly, but it is a house that we live in." The "we" consists of Cole and her husband, Art Robinson; her son Ethan; and always, a foreign exchange student or two.

The furnishings and inhabitants of Reynolds Cottage are as diverse and varied as the neighborhoods around it. To arrive at this grassy, tree-shaded

In the entrance hall, African-American art pairs with Victorian period furnishings.

106

compound of handsome brick buildings and a beautiful chapel, one must first drive through a housing project and some of the poorest sections in Atlanta. "I think it's important our students not forget that the majority of people who look just like them have substantially less than they have. And that's why we consciously must develop in our sisters a very deep sense of responsibility to others." Community service is strongly encouraged in the Spelman curriculum.

About the cultural context of her work and home, Cole is ambivalent. Only twenty-two percent of the students are from Georgia; the rest are from all over the nation and the world. And for them, the South, for better and for worse, holds a bit of a shock, from its dialects and slower pace of life, to more subtle aspects. "Though it is a national school, Spelman sits in the South and, in particular, in the warmth of *southern black culture*," she emphasizes, "and it is a warmth. One feels it immediately upon setting foot on this campus, from the guard at the gate to the maintenance man on the sidewalk, to the students. On the other hand, as an anthropologist I would say there are things which may not be immediately apparent. I mean, I think southerners, white and black, will often go through a lot to avoid conflict, so you sometimes have the feeling that you don't really know what they think or how they feel, because they're going to say the polite thing." As for Spelman's place in the larger community, in the city touted by its boosters as "too busy to hate?" "Well, my own view is that Atlanta isn't too busy to hate—all the time. Although for some of the time, I think it is. I think Atlanta is a very integrated, modern American city by day, and by night, it becomes a segregated city. Where people go home to, what restaurants they go to, whom they interact with, whom they entertain—all of that is too often color coded."

Old fears and foibles die hard, and the roots of tradition run deep in a city and region whose wealth and pride were once vested in little more. Atlanta's institutes of higher learning—Spelman and the Atlanta University Center, the Georgia Institute of Technology, Emory University, and others— are thriving proof of the power inherent in the demise of ignorance and the affirmation of "yes" to the question "Will you stick?"

The Druid Hills Residence of Wilma Stone

When famed Atlanta financier and developer Joel Hurt in 1892 commissioned Frederick Law Olmsted to plan Druid Hills, he conceived a "magnificent residential suburb" for "the handsomest residences in the South." Olmsted, who designed New York City's Central Park, is considered the father of American landscape architecture. Hurt, however, did not develop Druid Hills himself. He sold the nearly 1500-acre Druid Hills tract in 1908 for "a cool half million." *The Atlanta Journal* headline exclaimed, "LARGEST SALE EVER RECORDED HERE." Agreeing to fulfill Hurt's intentions and follow the Olmsted plan, the buyers were a consortium headed by Coca-Cola Company founder Asa G. Candler.

Situated northeast of downtown, the rolling, sylvan terrain is dotted with

small ponds and native flowering trees and shrubs, criss-crossed by winding, shaded streets. It is an idyllic setting for what are indeed among the South's "handsomest residences," by some of the best architects of the day. A Tudor house on Lullwater Road was the location for the movie *Driving Miss Daisy*, based on the Pulitzer Prize-wining play of the same name by Atlantan Alfred Uhry. Also Tudor, but on a grander scale, are *Callanwolde*, designed by Henry Hornbostle for Charles Candler, and *Lullwater House*, designed by Lewis E. Crook, Jr., for Walter Turner Candler. (*Lullwater* is

A French canapé nestles among books, pillows, porcelains and a collection of miniature bronzes, with a few dogs and a pheasant thrown in for good measure. All the mantels are original, this one adorned by a pair of 18th-century Meissen urns.

now the residence of the president of Emory University.) These Candlers were two of Asa's four sons, and Asa himself eventually moved from Inman Park to Druid Hills.

Another leading architect to grace Druid Hills was J. Neel Reid. By far the most influential early twentieth-century residential architect in Atlanta, Reid's work is perhaps best known for its classical and European inclinations, but not restricted to them. His was the standard by which the best was—and perhaps still is—defined. Reid was only 41 when he died in 1926, but his brief life's work is belied by his professional maturity, his mastery of architectural grace and subtlety, and his sheer prolificacy.

At age 28, commissioned by Walter Rich of the Rich's department store family, Reid designed the house in which Wilma Stone now lives. "It is reportedly the first house in Atlanta to have a swimming pool," Stone says. A collector and dealer of antiques, Stone has naturally become a student not only of the furniture and objects in her house, but of the house itself. "Neel Reid traveled extensively, and I think you can see in all of his designs a bit of Italy, a bit of England, a bit of France—that's what makes his houses so interesting." Stone was also attracted to the symmetry of the house. All the windows line up, and the identical wings recess. Inside, matching French doors lead from the central foyer to the living room on one side and dining room on the other. The rooms are large and the ceilings high, fortunately for the incurably acquisitive owner. "I love French antiques and collected quite a bit before I moved here from New Orleans. I still add to my collection, but it means I have to give up something because I don't have room for it."

This is true. The house is brimming if not bursting with furniture, accessories and artifacts, and one is hard-pressed to find credible Stone's claim of having given anything up. Neither nook nor cranny stands empty; nary a flat surface escapes unpaved with precious bibelots. Somehow she finds room for it, and the result is a feast for the eyes, even if one must squint occasionally at the glaring volume of it all. In the living room are no less than two sofas, one settee and a seventeenth-century French daybed, all laden with old tapestry pillows. Ten or so tables of various descriptions hold books and objects. Miniature bronzes, old photographs and figurines keep

company with all manner of gifts, favors and mementos like the ribboned remnants of a nosegay, from an occasion long past. Antique screens, Aubusson carpets, and paintings abound. Lighting the stairway are sconces of Venetian glass from an erstwhile ancient theater in Milan, possibly seventeenth century. There are more paintings and quite a dramatic, almost-life-sized portrait of Stone in a sort of Barbara Cartland-meets-Fannie Flagg flowing robe trimmed in ostrich feathers.

Stone came to Atlanta in 1969 and opened The Wrecking Bar in an his-

When a little bit too much is not enough: Wilma Stone's living room is a veritable museum of French antiques and bric-a-brac. The Louis XVI daybed heaped with old tapestry pillows was a rare find.

toric house on Moreland Avenue, specializing in architectural elements and antiques salvaged from old buildings. Coincidentally, it was the dawn of a strong preservation movement in Atlanta, a city which had not heard the alarm earlier, and had overslept, unaware that prized landmarks from the past had already been destroyed. Druid Hills, however, is an exception. Here, southern hospitality has been extended to history. Though some of the old houses were compromised when converted to duplexes or apartments, the active Druid Hills Civic Association, Stone, and others like her, are working to keep original architecture intact—and a gracious old neighborhood in good stead.

Stone is an incurable collector, but somehow she finds a place for it all.

Todd Murphy's Downtown Studio

Murphy's studio is a cavernous place, as it must be to accommodate the sculptures and massive works on canvas that have become his signature. Opposite: A chair and drop-cloth-draped sofa form a seating area under a huge conveyor belt. The Italian porcelain chandelier is reproduced in the painting behind it.

$\mathcal{T}$odd Murphy is an Atlanta artist whose star is fast ascending. He has exhibited on both coasts and in Europe. In Atlanta, he is represented by the Lowe Gallery on Bennett Street. His paintings and drawings have been acquired by important collectors and by famous ones: the High Museum in Atlanta; the Triton Museum in San Francisco; Michael Stipe, of the Athens-based rock band R.E.M.; boxer Sugar Ray Leonard; and pop music superstar (and part-time Atlanta resident) Elton John. One might think Murphy's paintbrush would point him toward a bigger city than Atlanta, or one with a more hip arts scene. But he was born and raised here, and here he'll stay.

"I think it's a very important place, the South, and becoming more so," says Murphy. "Anything you want to do you can do here. We have access to

all the same films, literature, any kind of media, Turner, CNN, all that stuff is here. It's a strange and wonderful place, and there's so much to write about and talk about. I know it's romanticized—the bad clichés you see on television—but people are also starting to understand that there's a depth in the South you don't find other places. There's a connection to the history of the South, to being southern. There are so many textures here. There is European history, black history, American Indian history. There's progress and there's poverty. There's open land and there's development. There's the growing international enterprise of a mega-city, and then there's all the old stuff, too. And we keep putting all these things on top of one another, and all that's fascinating."

Murphy's studio, appropriately, may be a piece of southern history itself. In a worn-down industrial district wedged between downtown, Oakland Cemetery, Inman Park and Cabbagetown, Murphy's ramshackle warehouse is one of the few ante-bellum buildings in the city. In his fiery rampage through Atlanta in 1864, General Sherman and his Union soldiers reportedly stabled their horses here, and, in so doing, spared the building. To pre-empt their Yankee opponents, however, the Confederates blew up the adjacent railroad and the ammunition-stocked depot nearby.

Today, the trains are running again, sounding as if they are going to rumble right through Murphy's studio. The floors shake. The advantage, though, is the tremendous, trackside loading dock which Murphy plans to turn into a sort of veranda, where he can be outside and where his dogs can romp. Inside, the beautiful old rose-colored brick and massive hand-hewn beams have been obscured by cinder blocks and steel girders. But it suited Murphy's need for big, raw space.

The first thing he built was a wall to enclose a darkroom. Next came the bedroom, then the stairs to the bathroom and loft, which sits atop the darkroom. Except for the heating system, he has done the construction himself. The furnishings he has scavenged from yard sales, flea markets and antique stores, and in some cases he has re-assembled them for uses other than those originally intended. The bed, for instance, is made from nineteenth-century English theater marquees and old wooden doors. A chest of drawers

The bath has the only window in Murphy's entire studio. An old claw-footed tub is topped with a plank to serve as makeshift easel for soaps and a sketchbook.

with the drawers removed becomes a bookcase. A desk is fashioned from a door and an old gate. An empty picture frame hung above it is a wink of irony, considering the context. An armchair from a yard sale is stripped of its upholstery and is a salute to retro-grunge-chic. Various pieces become props in his paintings, and some are consumed by his sculptures. It is a rustic improvisation with touches of civility—like Murphy's ever-present fresh flowers and fancy, handmade soaps and bath accessories. It is a decorative conundrum with style—part little boy's playhouse, part artist's haven.

People tell Todd Murphy that his studio looks like his paintings—large, looming, brooding, but also clever. They may be heavy and bold or light and delicate, complex, or startlingly simple. At one end of the warehouse looms a life-sized painting and photograph collage of a draft horse with the caption "PLOW." It is produced in the same body of work as a small charcoal line drawing of a goose, overlaid in gold leaf. Very different pieces of art from the same artist, but clearly, both works bear his signature—literal and figurative. His studio embraces this artistic contraposition with its enormous, dark cavern of working space, and the smaller, more human scale of the living area. "Whether it's working a painting or a space, it's all the same thing," he says. His art is where he lives.

Brooks Garcia's In-town Garden

This enchanting enclave flourishes on East Paces Ferry Road, a busy Buckhead thoroughfare and highly unlikely spot for a garden.

*N*o matter where I live, I have to garden," says Brooks Garcia, professional garden designer. Even though where he lives is more conducive to cultivating traffic jams than topiaries, that is precisely what he does—topiaries and more: vegetables, flowers and herbs galore. But it is an unlikely garden spot, to be sure. On the East Paces Ferry thoroughfare which links Piedmont and Peachtree roads, is a small, two-story, red brick apartment building where, amid the bustle, a garden grows.

It started about 1986, when Garcia moved in and did a bit of planting outside his entrance. Before long, a prospective tenant praised the apartment manager for the lovely blossoms, and the manager's enthusiasm flowered. The young plantsman was delighted, and at the slightest encouragement, he threw in the trowel. A veritable sod-cutting frenzy ensued. Out went the Bermuda and in came the fescue. He cleared out the scrub trees and fenced in the front, giving it the look of a cottage garden.

Inspired by a string of ideas as long as a clematis vine, Garcia built on the concept of a display garden he helped put together some years ago at the Atlanta Flower Show. That one was inspired by Rosemary Verey's potager garden in England, whose in turn was inspired by the famous potager at the Château de Villandry in the Loire Valley. Quite a noble lineage for a simple planting, if that was all it was to be; but of course it wasn't.

It was going to be beautiful, and edible as well. Garcia began by carving out flower beds and building arbors. Further structure and anchors are formed by evergreens and low fencing, and parsley and perpetual spinach line the central walkway and define borders. Planted for the entire growing season, the beds sprout perennial flowers, annuals, vegetables and herbs. In spring, old climbing roses—'New Dawn' and its parent, 'Dr. Van Fleet'—

cover the fences and frame one of the entrances to the apartments. There are elegant white trumpeter tulips, violas, dianthus and foxgloves. Hollyhocks, in the prettiest pastels, bloom in early summer. They were a gift from a stranger in London, where Garcia saw them growing, literally, out of a space in the sidewalk. He left a pleading note on the door of the house. Weeks later, he returned home to a waiting packet of seed accompanied by an apology that there were so few. So many had taken seeds already, the Brit bemoaned. Also in summer appear love-lies-bleeding (amaranthus), wild petunias, several varieties of salvias, four-o-clocks, angel trumpets (datura) and bidens, a native wildflower resembling yellow coreopsis that blooms until early fall.

The vegetables and herbs provide the apartment tenants with home-grown produce. Dragon tongue and bush beans, white eggplant, silver bullet corn, an Italian climbing squash called Tromboncino that can reach 30 to 40 feet in height with fruits two feet long, sixteen varieties of tomatoes and all kinds of cabbages begin the summer's bounty. (Alas, the gargantuan squash had little taste and was not re-planted the following season.) Some of the tomatoes entwine towers fashioned from the weedy "tree of heaven," or *Alanthus altissima*. There are antique French peas, four kinds of peppers, nasturtiums, dwarf zucchini, heads and heads of gourmet lettuces and old-fashioned bunching onions given him by a friend who has saved the sets for thirty years. Flowering herbs, herbs for cooking, and fragrant plants fill in everywhere else.

In fall and cold weather grow pansies, more parsley, and winter vegetables such as broccoli and Brussels sprouts. And watching over all year long are the topiaries, one in each of the four corners of the garden, representing the four seasons. Like giant birds perched on posts, the topiaries are fashioned from "common ol' privet," says Garcia, pleased to elevate such a humble but cooperative plant. All this, smack in the middle of town, "And still it's amazing," he says, "how many people walk by here every day and never even look up." To take time to smell the flowers, one must first find the garden. Brooks Garcia has found his, one of many he has created, but one of few for all to see, for the pleasure of merely passing by.

Garcia's apartment house garden from the window at a second floor landing. Sunflowers bob among the arbors covered with clematis, gourds and Mexican flame vine.

Left: A mixture of wild petunias, nasturtiums and Teddy Bear sunflowers spill over the picket fence.
Right: The splendid color and spindly tendrils of Malabar spinach make it a lovely climber.
Below: Assorted herbs and topiaries are divided by twig fencing, with fairy rose standards at each end. Gourd vines grow rampantly on the arbor above the bench.

Miss Mary's Garden at Capitol Homes

The golden dome of Georgia's Capitol gleams in the distance behind the Capitol Homes public housing complex. Opposite: Smith's walkway is a profusion of marigolds. Begonias and coleus in pots decorate the front steps.

*H*eading east through downtown, past well-dressed businessmen with places to go briskly striding along sidewalks laid across neatly trimmed grass, by skyscrapers and state buildings, Memorial Drive leads from prestigious executive offices to public housing projects. Capitol Homes, built in 1941, is just across the expressway. The unadorned, red-brick rows of apartments, with their tiny patches of yard, blend in to a presumably blighted urban tapestry. But not completely. Along the way, on the left, is a burst of color as gold and bright as the Capitol dome itself, and just as luminous in the sunshine.

Mary Smith's garden has many marigolds and butterflies, both of which slow passers-by and attract children, all of which she'll tell about—as she did one day to a perfect stranger who had been driving by and seen her garden—not that one could miss it. But it is difficult to hear her soft-spoken vernacular above the din of a nearby boom box and the roar of traffic just beyond her front stoop. "The children come over here and try to catch the butterflies, and I'll be lookin' out the window, and I say, 'Y'all better not go in Miss Mary's garden!'" They like to come, but they're scared I'll holler at 'em. So they just stand there and watch. They're right nice about it. They say, 'You sure do have some pretty flowers.'"

She always has. Reared in the time-honored, rural tradition of the swept yard, Smith has gardened since she was a child. "I'd sweep a clean place in the yard and make a playhouse. We'd get broken pieces of glass—anything we could find to put in it. And I'd get the prettiest weeds I could find and put all around it for my flowers. My grandmother had a vegetable garden and she'd give me some plants, and I'd set them out too." That was in Madison, Georgia, where she was born in 1917 and "raised up." She had a vegetable garden for a time in Atlanta, too, and claims, "Nobody ever bothered my collard greens until the night before Thanksgiving."

The only thing contrary about Mary may be her gumption. The question is not so much how her garden grows, but how it got there at all. Atlanta's public housing projects, though not without noble examples of urban pioneership, are generally not garden spots, *per se*. And Capitol Homes, where Mary Smith lives, is no exception. But her garden is—as are several others along her street, and more, scattered around the city. You just have to look.

A cactus supported by two broomsticks has grown for several years— not a species commonly cultivated out-of-doors in Atlanta.

Mary Smith's garden is a bright spot along the row of dark brick houses, defying the dullness of an inner city landscape. Zinnias, marigolds and the ferny foliage of cosmos are planted on one side.

Continuing east from Miss Mary's on Memorial Drive are Oakland Cemetery, Cabbagetown, Reynoldstown, and much Atlanta history, most unseen by tourists and townspeople alike, save for those who live there. But the touted "Atlanta spirit" lives in these places as well, flickering against a backdrop of poverty and struggle. And the personal triumphs seem to shine brighter there—as bright as Miss Mary's marigolds.

Ryan Gainey's Cottage Garden

The unmistakeable residence of Ryan Gainey, in Decatur. Old primroses interplanted with bellflowers border the sidewalk in front of the fence. Blooming behind it are a hearty red amaryllis, foxglove, and in the corner, Dame's Rocket hesperis.

There simply is nobody in this world like Ryan Gainey. Gardener, plantsman, designer, artist, epicure, philospher, Sybarite, son of the soil. He is a well-versed world traveler and a small-town Southern boy. He has been called visionary, prima donna, pain in the neck, and genius. And if the garden and the house are reflections of one's self, then Gainey's acre in Decatur is a paragon and a nonpareil.

The romantic cottage garden, as Gainey calls it, is self-expressive by nature, and idealized, evoking a sense of nostalgia. "When I came here it didn't look like this at all," he explains, "but I was inspired by the idea of a painting of a little tiny house in a setting with picket fences and arbors and vines and window boxes and things spilling over—sweet peas, nasturtiums, petunias, poppies, zinnias, old roses."

What he saw so clearly in his mind's eye has been carried out in a series of gardens, or garden rooms, each distinct. Some are restful and quiet, and some are busy, with riotous color and flowers and foliage spewing everywhere. Elements of English, French and Italian gardens meld into the environment of the American South. There is garden architecture and art and a bit of whimsy. No plant is more important than another. Each has its own beauty, its own story, its own heritage. Gainey has come to prefer simpler species and native plants to ostentatious hybrids, and he is as devoted to an unidentified wildflower found on a Tennessee roadside as he is to a rare cutting from a famous garden in France. The oak tree is as integral to the garden ambience as the red buckeye, hosta, and forest pansies beneath it. He cherishes the gangly chinaberry tree brought to him by a friend and exalts the common eleagnus, letting it have its way across an arbor made of sticks. This plant is "a rambunctious thing and often misused," he says, but working with it (letting it ramble and twine), instead of against it (clipping it and otherwise uglifying it), "you take full advantage of the plant and what it can do for you." He loves the beautiful silver backs of the leaves and the sweet fall fragrance of its tiny white blossoms.

Gainey bought the property in 1982 from a family of horticulturists who had operated a wholesale flower business there since 1919. With it he acquired the tiny house, several glass greenhouses, raised beds for flowers and herbaceous plants, sundry garden middens, and what used to be a barn out

The formal vegetable garden has fairy rose standards centered in boxwood diamonds. Big golden clumps of bidens and towering, self-branching sunflowers brighten the background. Plantings of herbs, vegetables and cutting flowers provide nearly all year long.

A view of the border garden from the rooftop porch. Flats of plants await setting out.

back. To one side of the house is a swept, dirt yard, a venerable icon of the rural southern vernacular which Gainey maintains here in homage to his childhood in the South Carolina sandhills. Ditto the chinaberry tree.

Beside the swept yard is the "visitor's garden," so-called because it is the first garden a visitor enters from the street, and there are many visitors. A shade garden, with its leafy green gloss and texture, lightly touched with cool color, this is a place of tranquillity, a respite. By contrast, the border garden is in constant commotion, always changing, always a show. Based on an ancient form, the border garden is divided into four quadrants, "like the four chambers of the heart," he says, with a center section, "being the center of one's own being." Filled with perennials, annuals, herbaceous plants, shrubs and grasses, it is a garden for all seasons.

From the sidewalk, through a *clair-voiette*, or sort of peephole, in the clipped cherry laurel hedge, one sees a small, round garden ringed in bright

golden barberry and *Sedum acre*. A pair of old terra-cotta urns atop pedestals fashioned from stacked flower pots marks the entrance to the oval garden. Adjacent to the border garden, the oval garden is a quieter, more secluded area with evergreens, foliage plants, Sweet Williams and Silver King artemisia around an allée carpeted in grass. Forming a border, in an almost childlike gesture, is a coping of tiny, upturned clay pots, hundreds of which Gainey inherited with the property.

At the opposite end of the oval garden are two unusual, upright boxwoods clipped into cone shapes. A pair of potted junipers are trained into spiral topiaries. Through these is passage to the vegetable garden, the most formal of all the garden rooms. Lettuces, cabbages, peas, *fraises des bois*, onions and beets are planted in and among three diamond-shaped boxwood parterres with a pink fairy tree rose in the middle of each. Orna-

**Left: Hollyhock, Joe and Rosemary recline on the master's bed.
Right: A collection of Gainey's signature straw hats are hung by the door.**

mental herbs are planted throughout, and the parterre is edged with golden thyme and cheerily punctuated with violas (Johnny-jump-ups) and a climbing Cecile Brunner rose. "This garden provides for the kitchen year round," Gainey says, "and it satisfies the farmer in me."

From there one wanders to the "barn" and into the tiny and slightly silly barn garden. "This is *Beulah Land*!" Gainey exclaims, waving at the assortment of cast-offs from the myriad parties and charity balls he has decorated for, his hodge-podge collection of "yard ornaments," old birdhouses, and stuff he found while just riding around in the country. "You have to satisfy this aspect of you if it's in you," he says. "And if you're a southerner, it's in you and you can't get away from it."

Among the salvaged treasures is a pale yellow iris which smells exactly like fresh grapefruit. Like many of the flowers and plants in Gainey's

Antique garden furniture in the breakfast room has a rustic elegance that dresses up or down with equanimity. The peeling plaster is left as it is, and the ceiling has been papered with the leaves of *Magnolia tripetala*, a deciduous variety.

garden, the citrus-scented iris was found in an old, abandoned garden. Others have been found in country fields, on building sites, around MARTA stations, and in cemeteries—his 'Oaklandia' rose, for example, was scavenged from Atlanta's Oakland Cemetery.

Considering the display of the immediate environs, it is not beyond the bounds of belief that a person might overlook the actual abode. An elderly man, whose daughter used to bring him to visit, once asked Gainey in all seriousness and surprise, "Oh, when'd you get a house?" "Well," answered he, "it's been there all along."

"You walk into the house as if it were another room in the garden," he says, "And then when you get there, there are other rooms." Built in 1906 of stone and heart pine, the house has retained its turn-of-the-century quaintness without becoming clichéd or too cute. A back porch creaks with old

This greenhouse is one of several, but the only one with a shower. Gainey maintains an aviary and small animal menagerie here, as well.

fashioned rockers, and the kitchen could be a picture on a 1920s biscuit tin. In the breakfast room the original paint and plaster has been left in a charming state of preserved peel and crumble. On the ceiling is a collage of leaves from the *Magnolia tripetala*, a deciduous magnolia he has growing in the shade garden. In the living room, removal of decrepit acoustical ceiling tiles revealed a geometric pattern painted long ago by the person who lived in the barn way back when. "He did all sorts of things," Gainey says. "He's the one who did the pond, the rock work and the little gazebo that used to be out there. Even the mailbox he built and set with the finial of a 1933 Pontiac."

The rustic quality so ingenuous in the garden is continued in the house. Gainey has antique wicker and garden furniture, a settee and chairs of bent willow, old trunks, wardrobes and linen presses. He drapes chairs and tables in fine old challis shawls, which are also part of his signature wardrobe, along with a broad-brimmed hat and, sometimes, an Indian necklace. Gainey's great-great grandmother was Cherokee, and his collection of native American baskets and pouches is testament to his atavistic admirations. He has also saved and framed a collection of hand-penciled notes written to his mother from his grandmother, who was quarantined in a tuberculosis camp and died at age 38. The notes included instructions in the delicate art of tatting, with samples enclosed. A montage of photographs, paintings, mementos and found objects resembles the garden enfolding it. Like the plants, each has a history, a story to tell, a heritage. And each resonates with some aspect of the owner's character.

The house, the garden, the man. In Gainey they are inseparable. Physically and philosophically symbiotic, they are his life, and his life's work. His shops, garden and floral design businesses, and his line of garden furniture and accessories come under the auspices of The Potted Plant, The Connoisseur's Garden and The Cottage Garden. His book, *The Well-Placed Weed*, was published in the fall of 1993 and accompanied a PBS series by the same name. He is pleased by his success but wary to keep it in perspective. "It's not what you're *going* to do, but what you have done *that day* that should fill up your life."

The Hughley Gallery in Reynoldstown

*N*ot every house is a home, in the conventional sense, but then "conventional" is a far cry from this story. It is not so much about decoration or design as it is about vision. And it is less about a personal, suburban aesthetic than about a communal, urban one. It is a story about courage, conception and rebirth in the city. And yes, it is about a house, its place in the unlikely context of this particular neighborhood, and the pioneering spirit of the man who bought it and fixed it up.

In 1986, native Atlantan and ex-New Yorker Young Hughley came home again. Three years later he bought this house, a run-down, "drug-infested den," he called it, in the heart of an historic but impoverished African-American community called Reynoldstown. At 142 Stovall Street, neighbors and passers-by gawked as walls were torn down and put up again, the roof was repaired, bold mustard yellow was spread on the outside, and carpet was laid on the inside. Trucks arrived bearing paintings and sculp-

ture. Then, in July of 1990, Hughley Gallery & Objects opened its doors. "A lot of people were skeptical about him opening an art gallery in this community," understates Mr. Hughley's wife Stephanie, the producing director of dance and theater for Atlanta's Cultural Olympiad and the former artistic director for the city's National Black Arts Festival. "I mean this is a place where the people live below the poverty level. People said you should go to Buckhead, or at least downtown. But this gallery became a cultural

Young Hughley behind his desk at the former Hughley Gallery, now home. The large charcoal, pencil and conté crayon work on paper is *Yo, Mary!*, by the Rev. Charlie Newton. To the right is a colored photograph by Lynn Marshall Linnemeier.

anchor in this community, and the community in turn adopted it. Every time there was an opening you'd see the kids and senior citizens coming, led by Young's mom. They wanted to learn about it; they wanted to know about this art." From an exhibition of painted photographs by Lynn Marshall Linnemeier, Mrs. Hughley recalls a piece featuring a young neighborhood woman and her baby, portrayed as Madonna and child. "Things like that made people in this community realize that art is not just a picture hanging on a wall in a rich person's house; it is an expression of our culture, and of our people, and they can relate to that." Speaking from experience, Mrs. Hughley says that for the first time in her life, "I saw an art institution in a community embrace the community." Even in hard times, she says, the Hughley Gallery was a "complete success, even if we had to close because it couldn't support itself financially." The payoff was more than money.

The spirit of the place—and the adventure in it—had captured the couple. So rather than leave Reynoldstown, they came to live in it. They gave up their house near Stone Mountain and gave the art gallery new life as a home. Mr. Hughley now is hopeful the revitalization efforts in the surrounding areas of Inman Park, Grant Park, and the once-infamous slum called Cabbagetown, will eventually edge toward Reynoldstown.

After the Civil War, a group of African-Americans, many of them freed slaves, had settled and begun to grow in the northwest part of Reynoldstown called "the slide" because it was near the railroad switching lines. And slowly, the surrounding whites sifted out. The Hughleys—Young's parents and eleven children—moved there in 1967, when Young had just graduated from high school. Today he is executive director of the Reynoldstown Revitalization Corporation. His parents and three brothers still live in Reynoldstown, and his father is chairman of the Reynoldstown Civic Improvement League.

The Hughley house is a beacon by way of example. "Some of the young people say they want to get out of here," Mr. Hughley once told a reporter for *The Atlanta Constitution*. "I say why run away? Make this better. That is what revitalization is all about. We have to make our own plans and sustain ourselves."

Dennis Schuhart's Bungalow in Peachtree Park

An 18th-century French console and a painted chair with spiral, fluted legs are both from the Louis XVI period. The miniature console is a cabinetmaker's sample, bought by Schuhart on his first buying trip to Paris.

$\mathcal{I}$t is interesting, if not odd, how Atlanta has developed. Quiet, woodsy residential areas are mere steps away from multi-lane motorways and roaring traffic. Quaint, older neighborhoods huddle in the shadows of skyscrapers. It is fortunate that this fast-growing city hasn't burst all its pockets of small town ambiance, and the neighborhood preservationists fight to keep it that way. One place which seems safe (for the time being, anyway) is Peachtree Park in north Atlanta. A few blocks from Lenox Square, in the foothills of the black, mountainous Atlanta Financial Center, this modest little enclave speaks of front porches and American flags, where older folks have lived for a long time, and where young professionals are just starting out.

When designer Dennis Schuhart looked here, the 1920s Arts and Crafts style bungalow he found did not especially appeal. "But what did appeal," he says, "were the tall ceilings, and the size and shape of the rooms, which are almost square. It is well-balanced and the scale is nice." So Arts and Crafts bungalow it is. He bought it from the original owner, who was ninety-three years old and who had been the first woman stockbroker in Atlanta. And everything in the house was pink and green ". . . right down to the foil paper in the dining room," says Schuhart. "In its way, it had a lot of style."

But a decorator must decorate. And yet, Schuhart admonishes, "I don't ever want it to look like it's *decorated.*" He also did not want it to look like a cottage, although essentially that is what it is. "I didn't want the expected look when you walked into the house. I just wanted it to be understated and classical in taste, with a mixture of Empire, Louis XVI and Directoire styles, but not the really high styles of any of those. With the kind of furniture I have, it never would have worked if I'd taken it too seriously."

As there is no entrance hall or foyer, save for the screened front porch,

one steps from the porch directly into the living room. This wouldn't do. "So instead of arranging it like a living room, I put a big round table there, which makes it feel sort of like an entrance hall. The fireplace gives it warmth, and I think the way the chairs are casually arranged around the room makes it an area where you can easily have a conversation." And then he also uses it as a dining room—the room in many houses which most readily lends itself to other use, since its formal role is called for rather infrequently.

Such nimble solutions to everyday design challenges are Schuhart's stock-in-trade. Something of a *wunderkind* in the Atlanta design world, he was hired by preeminent Atlanta designer and antiques dealer Dotty Travis as soon as he completed his design degree at the Art Institute of Atlanta. Holding forth at the Travis & Co. showroom in the Atlanta Decorative Arts Center, Schuhart has built a reputation for sound advice and utterly creative approaches to interiors. His vignette and window displays—not to mention his flower arrangements—are the stuff of ADAC legend. And they are the designer's invitation to indulge his eccentric tastes and touches of wildness, splashing about exotic motifs and lush fabrics.

At home, however, he is more subtle. His living room (the dining room in the house's former life) is an intimate sitting room. Between a pair of comfortable upholstered chairs, a Louis XVI commode sits beneath an Empire

mirror once gilded, now stripped, with an antique English bullseye mirror above that. Also stripped are the walls, down to the cracked and green-mottled plaster, which Schuhart decided he liked and left that way. Only the trim is painted, and the wall below the chair rail is covered in cork. The juxtaposition of textures is ingenius. Books are stacked about on ottomans and under consoles, and unusual accessories go a long way toward avoiding predictability: a gourd perched on a glass vase, a large hornet's nest, bunches of glass grapes, a silk bean bag, massive stone flower and fruit baskets he bought at an estate sale.

Just beyond the living room is a tiny alcove off the kitchen where Schuhart has coffee, chats on the phone, does paper work. The morning sun streams through the matchstick shades and sparkles on the glass-topped

A French chair in ivory damask and a marble-topped Louis XVI console occupy a corner of the entrance hall and dining room. Schuhart collects *tabourets,* **or miniature ottomans, like the leopard-covered one here. The alabaster lamp he found in Paris.**

A 19th-century Aubusson, unusual for its Greek key border and colors, anchors the casual seating arrangement around a marple-topped Louis XVI commode and a book stack that might double as a small coffee table.

table. He'll have supper there, too, unless he's entertaining. "If I have more than three people for dinner, we'll eat in the entrance," he says, instead of calling it the "dining room." He entertains informally fairly often, but his Fourth of July party is a favorite. Urban sprawl has its advantages: Schuhart's back yard commands a great view of the fireworks shot from Lenox Square. "And I fill that front table with fabulous desserts and food." Does he cook, too? "No," he says, "I decorate."

Eve Davis's Garden

$\mathscr{E}$ve's Garden," as it is painted in script on the yellow tin mailbox, grows in an offbeat southeast section of Atlanta which might be called Lakewood, near the Lakewood park and amphitheater and south of Grant Park. Although less than ten minutes from downtown, the area has a rural character. Narrow, country roads wind by small houses with big front porches. Children play in yards that double as parking lots for tricycles and wagons. Horticulturist and floral designer Eve Davis reckons about half her neighbors are African-American and half are white. As Atlanta neighborhoods go, it is modest; but for Davis, it is perfect. She had searched intently for months for a house, and when she saw this one, she knew. She had, literally, seen it in her dreams.

An ancient (for Atlanta) frame structure, going to seed in an overgrown

Once part of a large farm, the 1867 house was built by a Civil War veteran. Opposite: Queen Anne's lace and the daisy-like feverfew are a delicate blanket of white, punctuated with yarrow and lychnis.

bower of green, the house is dated 1867 and was first lived in by a Civil War veteran named Burrows. It is a classic, old southern design, with four large rooms divided by an ample central foyer. "This used to be a large farm," Davis points out. "And all the land around here belonged to it. There had been a garden here once, but it hadn't been taken care of in a long time."

No sooner had Davis moved in than she set about planting another, reviving a beauty that had long laid fallow. At the time, the former Montessori School teacher was working as a fabric artist, but she soon channeled her efforts into work which embraced her creative talents as well as her horticultural training from Clemson University. "As an artist I've worked in different mediums," she explains. "I create a vision in the mind's eye, then bring it into the physical plane. I love the temporal quality of floral design and the subtle combinations of color." And yet, she says, "Gardening has always been the passion of my life. I've been gardening since I could walk. I've often wondered if I'm not part plant." A native of Charleston, South Carolina, Davis's first conscious memory is of being in her mother's garden. By the time she was 10, she had taken it over completely, while her mother moved on to hybridizing camellias and azaleas.

Bright-blossoming sweet peas trail along a picket fence.

Years later, taking inspiration from a suburban Charleston woman who sold cut flowers for teas and weddings, Eve's initial idea for a gardening venture was to create a similar business. The enterprise grew into an extensive nursery specializing in perennials and annuals, and a flourishing floral design business.

Hers is a classic cottage garden, where flowers tumble into pathways, ramble on trellises and trail along picket fences. The main part of the garden is a profusion of beautiful blossoms, spindly stems, and foliage like lace trimming. "I like the little edging things," she says, "so I have lots of different kinds of dianthus." She is particularly fond of one pale pink variety, local to the neighborhood. She has come to call it "Eve's dianthus," as no one has been able to identify it otherwise. Also local, in fact growing on her property when she acquired it, is a deep blue Siberian iris, "almost navy blue," she says. "I haven't seen another one like it." Annuals include forget-me-nots, baby blue eyes, Johnny-jump-ups, larkspur, nasturtiums, a pleth-

Left: New Dawn roses spill over an arbor into a sumptuous assortment of spring flowers: daisies, columbine, cleome, poppies, cornflowers and dianthus.
Right: A misty morning creates a fairytale setting in Eve Davis's romantic cottage garden. A deep purple _Clematis jackmanii_ crowns the fence with English daisies, violas, poppies and Sweet Williams.

ora of poppies—Shirleys in splashy colors—and many kinds of violas and pansies—Eve's professed favorites. Spring bulbs are scattered under trees and throughout the garden. Old fashioned perennials include foxglove, columbine, veronica, old roses, Sweet Williams, and Shasta daisies of every description that bloom from spring until fall.

Another garden nearer the house contains an artful combination of vegetables, herbs and flowers. Flower borders near the greenhouse bloom from early spring until hard frost. A kitchen garden grows "every conceivable herb, especially the culinary herbs," Davis says. "I love herbs and I use them every day. I cook with them, and I use them in almost every arrangement I do. For instance, I always put rosemary—for remembrance—in bridal bouquets and in the groom's boutonnieres." A variety of lettuces bring another dimension of texture and color. "The black-seeded Simpson is especially beautiful," says Davis. "I even mix it in the flower borders." The deep fuchsia of radicchio, the reds, purples, and greens of cabbage, the pale tones of celery, the soft white of crisp cauliflower, and the deep, dusty tones of spinach and beets are a harmonizing palette of nature's bounty.

"This is a highly personal garden," she says, "and it's very much a romantic cutting garden. One of the comments I hear most is that it looks like I just threw out some seeds and they came up where they were. I love that because it's just what I intended."

Index